First Timothy

First Timothy

By

D. EDMOND HIEBERT

MOODY PRESS

CHICAGO

ISBN: 0-8024-2054-0

Printed in the United States of America

Contents

Preface

THIS STUDY of I Timothy is intended to present a concise yet
precise interpretation of the apostle's thought in the letter.
The reader is urged to keep a copy of the scriptural text open
before him. The text quoted is that of the American Standard
Version (1901), but the interpretation is based on a study of
the original Greek. Technical matters in connection with the
language of the original have been kept to a minimum, and
Greek words, whenever referred to, have been transliterated
into the English.

The material of this slender volume constitutes a verse-by-
verse interpretation of I Timothy, but it is not cast into the form
of a series of comments on the numbered verses of the scriptural
text. In an effort to keep the trend of thought clearly before the
reader, an outline of the epistle is inserted into the interpretation
and made the guide in the development of the exposition. It is
hoped that thus the line of the apostle's thought will not become
lost in a maze of details, a danger not infrequently encountered
under the ordinary practice of simply commenting on the verses
seriatim.

Limitations of space have prevented an elaboration of the
interpretation given. Homiletical applications have of necessity
been largely dispensed with. Where different views as to the
meaning of the text have been advanced, I have usually simply
set down what I consider to be the right interpretation without

enumerating all the divergent views on the matter. Such a practice is a favorite with certain commentators but it is a weariness to the flesh for the ordinary reader.

I owe much to others who have labored on this important letter. My indebtedness will be evident from the Bibliography.

An Introduction to I Timothy

THE TERM "the Pastoral Epistles" is used to designate the triad of epistles addressed to Timothy and Titus. Although addressed to individuals, they are not exclusively personal and private communications, like Philemon. They were addressed to men who stood in places of important ecclesiastical responsibility at the time Paul wrote to them. I Timothy and Titus especially have an official character which marks them as being more than personal letters to Paul's friends. Since the letters are largely concerned with matters of church order and discipline, the term "Pastoral Epistles" is quite appropriate. They occupy a classical position in the Christian church as a guide for the "good soldier" of Jesus Christ in the Christian warfare. They offer much that is of highest significance to the Christian pastor today.

However, the modern implications of the term "pastoral" must not lead us to a misinterpretation of the position of the men to whom these letters were addressed. They were not pastors of local churches in the modern sense of that term. Titus was not the pastor of the Cretan churches, nor was he the first bishop of the church on Crete. That he did not hold a permanent office in the churches of Crete the letter clearly indicates (3:12). Nor was Timothy the pastor of the church at Ephesus. The Ephesian church already had its own organization of "elders" long before Timothy was stationed there (Acts 20:17-35). He was stationed at Ephesus as Paul's personal representative, working with all the churches of the region. His task was to direct, organize, and supervise the work of the churches and to help repel and eject certain errorists whose efforts were threatening to corrupt that work. He had been temporarily left behind to carry on the work which Paul would do if he were there himself.

All three of these epistles claim to be written by the apostle Paul. Down through the centuries the Christian church has always regarded them as genuine products of that illustrious apostle. But during the past century and a half the Pauline authorship of these epistles has been fiercely assailed.

The force of the external historical evidence is all in favor of the traditional view concerning their authorship. The witness of the early Christian church to their place in the New Testament canon and their Pauline authorship is as clear, full, and unhesitating as that given to the other epistles. Even those who reject the Pauline authorship must admit that there is much in their contents that is characteristically Pauline. This fact has led some scholars to the compromise position that they contain considerable Pauline fragments but that the present epistles are not the work of Paul. This position is untenable. The subjective criteria of the critics produce no agreement as to what is truly Pauline in them. If some follower of Paul composed them and passed them off as the work of Paul, then they are a forgery and must be rejected as a pious fraud.

All critical objections to the Pauline authorship of these epistles are based entirely on internal and theoretical grounds. The attack has been directed along chronological, ecclesiastical, doctrinal, and linguistic lines, which need not be elaborated here.

The conservative position continues to hold the favor of many able scholars and is again receiving wide support in critical circles. We see no compelling reason to abandon the traditional view that these epistles are the genuine products of Paul's old age. "The second century never spoke as these Epistles speak" (quoted in Gurney).

It is obvious that II Timothy stands last among the Pastoral Epistles. It is the last extant writing from the pen of Paul. As he wrote he was again in prison, was regarded as a malefactor, and was facing imminent death. But I Timothy and Titus, as companion epistles, reflect a different situation. There is no hint that Christianity has yet been declared an illegal religion by the emperor. In them Paul is seen again busily engaged in missionary labors. He is free to move about at will and to plan his own activities. That they belong to the time following his release from the first Roman imprisonment seems clear.

The occasion for the writing of I Timothy is apparent from the Epistle. Upon his return to Ephesus, following his release at Rome, Paul discovered that during his absence Ephesus had become a storm center of false teaching. It was a sad fulfillment of the prediction he had made to the Ephesian elders about five years before (Acts 20:29, 30). He dealt personally with the leaders of the trouble (1:19, 20). When Paul found it necessary to leave Ephesus for Macedonia, he left Timothy at Ephesus to deal with the situation in his behalf. When he wrote this letter to Timothy he hoped to return before long, but in case he was delayed the letter would supply the need of Timothy. His realization that Timothy had a difficult task to perform and that he needed encouragement and written authorization to carry out the work entrusted to him caused him to write.

Paul appears to have been in Macedonia at the time of writing, but he may possibly have gone on to Greece. He urges Timothy to remain at Ephesus as he had been requested.

The Epistle must be dated after Paul's release from the first Roman imprisonment in the spring of A.D. 63. The exact date assigned to it will largely depend upon the reconstruction of Paul's journeys following his release. The general practice is to place these epistles as near the end of Paul's life as possible. But since I Timothy and Titus, unlike II Timothy, contain no hint that Christianity had yet been declared an illegal religion by the Roman government, it seems best to date it before the outbreak of the Neronian persecution which began in the fall of the year A.D. 64. Our view is that it was written during the same year that Paul was released from prison, hence we suggest the date as the early fall of the year A.D. 63.

The purpose of the Epistle may be viewed from Paul's concern for Timothy personally, as well as his concern for the welfare of the Asian churches generally.

Addressed to Timothy personally, the Epistle was intended to give him needed assistance in the performance of the difficult task which had been entrusted to him. The opposition which Timothy faced in his work made it desirable that he be given some explicit authorization, beyond that of a mere verbal commission, to enable him for a longer period to exercise the authority wherewith Paul had invested him. This Epistle would give Timothy some documentary proof of his authorization to act as the apostle's representative. Accordingly much of the Epistle is directly occupied with the personal life and activities of Timothy himself.

In writing, Paul also had the larger interests of the churches in Asia in mind. The presence of numerous false teachers with their pernicious teachings constituted a serious threat to the churches. Timothy had been left behind to check the evil influences of these men (1:3-7). The welfare of the churches demanded that these troublers be dealt with. But Timothy was also to perform a constructive task in the churches. He was to aid them by giving guidance concerning public worship, assisting in the selection of proper church leaders, and overseeing the spiritual affairs of the churches. It was a huge task for a young man like Timothy. This letter was written to encourage and assist him in the worthy fulfillment of that task.

An Outline of I Timothy

THE SALUTATION, 1:1, 2
1. The Writer, v. 1
2. The Reader, v. 2a
3. The Greeting, v. 2b

I. THE CHARGE TO TIMOTHY CONCERNING FALSE
TEACHERS, 1:3-20

1. The Charge to Timothy to Preserve the Purity of the Gospel, vv. 3-11
   a. The nature of the charge, vv. 3, 4
      1) The impartation of the charge, v. 3a
      2) The contents of the charge, vv. 3b, 4
   b. The aim of the charge, v. 5
   c. The reason for the charge, vv. 6-11
      1) The failure of the false teachers, vv. 6, 7
      2) The true knowledge concerning the law, vv. **8-11**
         a) The nature of the law, v. 8
         b) The purpose of the law, vv. 9, 10
         c) The harmony of this view with the Gospel, v. 11
2. The Apostle's Thanksgiving for His Relation to the Gospel, vv. 12-17
   a. The thanksgiving for his appointment to God's service, v. 12

13

      1) The desirability of the office, v. 1
      2) The qualifications for the office, vv. 2-7
        a) The first seven qualifications, v. 2
        b) The second seven qualifications, vv. 3-6
        c) The qualification as to community standing, v. 7
    b. The qualifications for deacons, vv. 8-12
      1) The personal qualifications of the deacons, vv. 8, 9
      2) The testing of deacons, v. 10
      3) The qualifications of the women (deaconesses),
        v. 11
      4) The domestic qualifications of deacons, v. 12
    c. The reward of faithful service, v. 13
  3. The Personal Word to Timothy in View of Christian
    Truth, 3:14-16
    a. The purpose in writing to Timothy, vv. 14, 15a
    b. The nature of the church, v. 15b
    c. The substance of Christian truth, v. 16

III. THE ADVICE TO TIMOTHY IN VIEW OF THE
    CHARGE, 4:1-6:2

  1. His Personal Work in View of the Apostasy, 4:1-16
    a. The objective warning against false teaching, vv. 1-5
      1) The prediction of the apostasy, v. 1a
      2) The characterization of the apostates, vv. 1b, 2
      3) The teaching of the apostates, vv. 3-5
        a) The nature of the teaching, v. 3a
        b) The refutation of the teaching, vv. 3b-5
    b. The subjective fortification against error, vv. 6-16
      1) The fortification through a faithful ministry,
        vv. 6-11
        a) The characteristics of a good minister, v. 6
        b) The activity of a good minister, vv. 7-9
          (1) Neg.—The refusal of myths, v. 7a

    (2) Pos.—The exercising of himself unto godliness, vv. 7b-9
   c) The motivation of the good minister, v. 10
   d) The duty of the good minister, v. 11
  2) The fortification through becoming conduct as a minister, vv. 12-16
   a) The indication of his personal duties, vv. 12-14
    (1) To make his youth respected because of his example, v. 12
    (2) To attend to the public services, v. 13
    (3) To exercise his gift, v. 14
   b) The exhortations diligently to fulfill these duties, vv. 15, 16

2. His Official Work with Various Groups, 5:1-6:2
 a. The attitude in dealing with individual members, 5:1, 2
 b. The duty in regard to widows, 5:3-16
  1) The duty of supporting widows, vv. 3-8
   a) The command to honor genuine widows, v. 3
   b) The definitive classification of widows, vv. 4-6
    (1) The widow having children, v. 4
    (2) The widow who is a genuine widow, v. 5
    (3) The widow living in pleasure, v. 6
   c) The instructions concerning parental support, vv. 7, 8
  2) The instructions concerning the enrollment of widows, vv. 9-15
   a) The qualifications of those enrolled, vv. 9, 10
   b) The rejection of the young widows, vv. 11-13
    (1) The command to reject the young widows, v. 11a
    (2) The reasons for the rejection, vv. 11b-13
   c) The apostolic directive for young widows, vv. 14, 15
  3) The duty of a believing woman, v. 16

c. The duty toward elders, 5:17-25
   1) The duty of honoring good elders, vv. 17, 18
     a) The statement of the duty, v. 17
     b) The substantiation of the duty, v. 18
   2) The instructions concerning the trial of an elder, vv. 19-21
     a) The caution in receiving an accusation against an elder, v. 19
     b) The judgment upon the sinning, v. 20
     c) The impartiality in the judgment, v. 21
   3) The advice concerning the ordination of elders, v. 22
   4) The suggestion concerning Timothy's use of a little wine, v. 23
   5) The enunciation of principles for testing candidates, vv. 24, 25

d. The instructions concerning the slaves, 6:1, 2
   1) The duty of slaves toward unbelieving masters, v. 1
   2) The duty of the slave of a believer, v. 2a
   3) The duty of Timothy to teach these things, v. 2b

IV. THE CONCLUDING INSTRUCTIONS AND EXHORATIONS TO TIMOTHY, 6:3-21a

1. The Description of the False Teacher, vv. 3-5
  a. The identification of the false teacher, v. 3
  b. The verdict on the false teacher, vv. 4, 5
2. The Relation of Godliness and Wealth, vv. 6-10
  a. The gain of true godliness, vv. 6-8
    1) The gain of godliness with contentment, v. 6
    2) The nature of godly contentment, vv. 7, 8
  b. The danger to those seeking wealth, vv. 9, 10
    1) The nature of the danger, v. 9
    2) The reason for the danger, v. 10a

An Interpretation of I Timothy

THE SALUTATION, 1:1-2.

IT WAS THE STANDARD PROCEDURE in the first century for the writer of a letter to begin with his own name and then write the name of the recipient; some form of greeting was added. This practice was followed in official correspondence as well as in private communications. And the ancient practice certainly was more logical than our modern method. Who today ever reads a letter without first turning to the signature at the close?

The salutation consists of the usual three members: the name of the writer in the nominative, the name of the reader in the dative, and the greeting as an exclamatory nominative. Paul's amplification of all three members in this salutation reflects the contents and purpose of the letter. Its very tone indicates that the letter is both personal and official.

1. The Writer, v. 1

The writer designates himself as "Paul." The name is from the Latin *Paulus,* meaning little. His Hebrew name was "Saul." As the son of a Jewish father who was also a Roman citizen, it is very probable that he received both names at birth. It was a common practice among the Jews to have both a Jewish and a Gentile name. In the Book of Acts, Luke always uses the name "Saul" until Acts 13:9; but after that always "Paul." "Saul" was appropriately used as long as his life and activities were intimately connected with things Jewish, but when his work among the Gentiles became prominent his Gentile name was appropriate. As the apostle to the Gentiles he always uses his Gentile name in his epistles.

Paul indicates his official position by calling himself "an apostle of Christ Jesus." The term "apostle," coming from the verb *apostellō*, means "one who is sent forth" and carries the thought of official and authoritative sending with the necessary equipment. The term is here used in its usual narrow sense describing Paul as one called to the apostolic office, like the Twelve, and invested with its authority. The added genitive, "of Christ Jesus," indicates whose apostle he is. His apostleship was derived from and relates to Christ Jesus.

The manuscripts vary in the order in the compound name. The order "Christ Jesus," followed in the American Standard Version has stronger manuscript support than the reverse order of the King James Version. Both orders are common to Paul, but the order "Christ Jesus" prevails in the later epistles. The average English reader uses either order merely to identify the Person to whom reference is made without any clear consciousness of a difference in meaning. But to Paul and his Greek readers each order had its own significance. In either order the first member of the compound name indicates whether the theological or the historical idea concerning our Lord is chiefly in the writer's mind.

The order "Christ Jesus" emphasizes the theological fact that the One who was with the Father in eternal glory became incarnate in human form. In his writings Paul uses either order, but the order "Christ Jesus" predominates. Perhaps this is because Paul had not accompanied the human Jesus while He was here on earth and in his own experience the knowledge of the Christ of glory came first. (According to the Greek text of Westcott and Hort, in this Epistle Paul uses "Christ Jesus" twelve times and "Jesus Christ" only twice.)

By calling himself "an apostle of Christ Jesus," Paul stresses the fact that the Christ of glory who became incarnate to become our Saviour had called and commissioned him as His messenger. Such was the nature of his office.

Paul was ever conscious of the fact that his apostolic office was not due to his personal choice but rather that he had been divinely entrusted with it. It came as a direct commission from God and was not of human origin. He accordingly describes his apostleship as being "according to the commandment of God our Saviour, and Christ Jesus our hope." The word "command" is a military term and denotes an injunction or order that must be obeyed. The call to be an apostle came to him as a divine command which must be obeyed. His apostolic activity and authority were in accordance with that command. Paul yielded unhesitating obedience to that command so that he could say: "I was not disobedient unto the heavenly vision" (Acts 26:19). Are we so prompt to obey the call of God upon our lives?

This command he presents as proceeding equally from God and Christ Jesus. It was the command "of God our Saviour, and Christ Jesus our hope." The application of the term "saviour" to the Father is peculiar to the Pastoral Epistles in the writings of Paul. (The thought is common in the Old Testament and the expression is used in Luke 1:47 and Jude 25.) In his earlier epistles Paul uses it only of Christ (Eph. 5:23; Phil. 3:20). In the Pastoral Epistles he applies the term to the Father six times (I Tim. 1:1; 2:3; 4:10; Titus 1:3; 2:10; 3:4) and to Christ four times (Titus 1:4; 2:13; 3:6; II Tim. 1:10). However, the conception of salvation originating with God the Father is common to his earlier epistles (cf. Col. 1:13; I Cor. 1:21; II Cor. 5:19). This peculiarity of language may well be regarded as an indication of the genuineness of these epistles, for it seems highly improbable that a forger would so strikingly depart from Paul's previous usage.

The command is viewed as also coming from "Christ Jesus

our hope." (The insertion of the term "Lord" in the King James Version follows an inferior reading.) The language is again exceptional when he describes Christ Jesus as "our hope." But this use of an abstract term to designate a person is in accord with Ephesians 2:14 where Paul speaks of Christ as "our peace."

What a blessed realization is the truth that Christ Jesus is "our hope." Not only that He gives us hope, but He *is* our hope. He is the hope of the individual and of the world; personally, nationally, and internationally. He is our hope in every sense of the term, the object, the author, the foundation, the substance of our hope.

In speaking of God as "Saviour" and of Christ Jesus as our "hope," Paul is not thinking of the relation of the Persons in the Godhead to each other but of their relations to believers. The Father is the fountain of our salvation and Christ Jesus is the embodiment of our hope. The Father is appropriately called "our Saviour" since He is the ultimate source and fount of human salvation. The title is equally appropriate to Christ Jesus as the One in whom that salvation was wrought in human history. Because of His work of redemption Christ Jesus is now our hope, our hope for past sins forgiven, our hope for present victory, our hope for future glory. The use of the appropriate "our" with both the Father and Christ speaks of the believer's acceptance and confession of a personal relation to both. And the use of the plural, rather than the singular "my," indicates the consciousness of our fellowship with other believers in these glorious possessions.

The union of Christ Jesus with the Father in this commission of Paul as an apostle is clear evidence of Paul's conviction concerning the true deity of Christ. If in his thinking Christ was merely a creature, however excellent, thus to unite the two Persons is inconceivable for one with the strong monotheistic background of Paul.

This assertion, in the very salutation, of the writer's apostolic authority is indicative of the contents of the letter. It is not simply a note of personal friendship. It is addressed to Timothy as the apostle's personal representative at Ephesus. While addressed to him personally, the letter has an official character. It is intended to certify to the churches with whom Timothy is dealing that the instructions it contains are authoritative and that Timothy is authorized to act as the delegate of Paul himself.

2. The Reader, v. 2a

The recipient of the letter is named and briefly described. "To Timothy, my true child in faith."

The name of Timothy is familiar to every reader of the New Testament. He was one of Paul's most devoted and constant companions. His name occurs seventeen times in ten different Pauline Epistles, more often than any other companion of Paul. And two of the letters which make up the last group of Paul's epistles are addressed to him. His prolonged and intimate association with Paul has lastingly associated his name with that illustrious apostle.

Paul addresses Timothy as "my true child in faith." This seems clearly to imply that Timothy was Paul's own convert, although there is no word in the original to represent the "my" in our translation. Paul calls Timothy his "child" (*teknon*), rather than "son" as the King James Version has it. The latter would have carried with it the idea of Timothy's maturity and responsibility, while the former conveys the thought of tenderness and endearment. The word for "own" in the King James is *gnēsios* and means "lawfully begotten, true, genuine." As a "genuine child" Timothy is running true to his spiritual parentage, showing real and marked resemblance to his father. Their relationship existed not in the physical but in the spiritual realm. Paul had begotten him in the realm of "faith." The absence of the article with "faith" in the Greek leaves it an open question as to whether we should render it "the faith," thus denoting the objective content of the Christian revelation, or simply "faith," meaning the subjective principle of personal faith. Either view is possible from the standpoint of Pauline usage.

3. The Greeting, v. 2b

The greeting is characteristically Pauline and distinctively Christian. "Grace, mercy, peace, from God the Father and Christ Jesus our Lord." The conventional form of the time simply added "greeting" to the preceding two members of the salutation. Illustrations of this practice are found in the New Testament from the pen of a non-Christian (Acts 23:26), as well as Christian writers (Acts 15:23; James 1:1). This commonplace greeting Paul replaces in his letters with a wish indicative of the heart of the Christian faith. The form may well be original with Paul. The greeting indicates both the content of the apostle's fervent wish for Timothy and the source to which he looks for its fulfillment.

His wish for his beloved Timothy is "grace, mercy, peace." The distinctive feature here and in II Timothy 1:2 is the insertion of "mercy" between the grace and peace used elsewhere. (Its insertion in the salutation to Titus lacks manuscript authority.) This invocation of a threefold blessing upon the reader occurs elsewhere only in II John 3, written years later. This interesting variation in the Pauline greeting, rather than disproving the Pauline authorship of these epistles, is a strong proof of their genuineness. What forger would have dared to make such an innovation in the salutation without a precedent for it? It is much more natural to think that the keen solicitude of the aged apostle for his young friend in his difficult position led him to insert the additional prayer for mercy as springing from his own enlarged experience of divine mercy.

This threefold invocation comprehends all the blessings which come to us now through the Gospel. "Grace" is the undeserved favor of God toward the guilty sinner, removing the guilt of his past sins and relieving him of deserved punishment. "Mercy" is the self-moved, spontaneous compassion of God for the miserable and distressed, freeing the sinner from the consequent misery of his sins. The believer stands in constant need of the continued experience of both. "Grace is multiplied for God's children in a constant shower of undeserved gifts (John 1:16, 'grace for grace'), and so mercy continues in ever new deliverance out of trouble" (Lenski). "Peace" is the state of salvation which results from God's grace and mercy. It speaks of the harmony which results from the removal of the discord which sin has produced. A feeling of well-being and tranquillity follow. What richer blessings could one desire for another than these? " 'Grace, mercy and peace' are the triple blessings of the Christian life, as faith, hope and charity are the triple fruit of the Christian character" (Lilley).

This triple blessing Paul thinks of as coming "from God the Father and Christ Jesus our Lord." Both are involved in the bestowal of these gifts. Christ is coupled with the Father as the source of blessing in all the Pauline salutations except in Colossians where, in the critical text, we have only "from God our Father." The government of the two Persons under one preposition intimately unites them. This close union of Christ with the Father in the commission of the apostle in verse 1 and here, as the source of the triple blessings desired for Timothy, necessarily involves His coequal deity with the Father. Only One who is truly God can stand in such relations and fulfill such offices as here indicated.

In invoking these blessings upon his spiritual son, Timothy, Paul looks first to "God the Father," the source of all fatherhood (Eph. 3:15). As members of the family of God we can confidently look up to the Father for all our needs. Next to the Father, Paul places the name of Christ Jesus as the source of these blessings. All the Father's gifts come to us through the

Son. Notice that this is the third time the name of Christ Jesus occurs in this salutation. How Paul loved that adorable name! Paul and Timothy are each named once, the Father is named twice, but Christ Jesus is named thrice. He is the very heart and center of Christianity. But He is now designated, not as Son in contrast to the Father, but as "our Lord." While we gratefully worship God as our Father we also bow before Christ Jesus as "our Lord." To acknowledge Him as Lord is to own and obey His authority over us. Again notice the appropriative "our." Is he truly "our Lord" in practical daily living? It has well been said:

> If you do not crown Him Lord of all,
> You do not really crown Him Lord at all.

I. THE CHARGE TO TIMOTHY CONCERNING
FALSE TEACHERS, 1:3-20

CHAPTER 1, constituting the first main division of the Epistle, deals with the first duty laid upon Timothy as the apostolic representative at Ephesus. He is to check the false teachers at work in and around Ephesus. The chapter falls into three paragraphs. Paul states the substance and details of the charge to Timothy (vv. 3-11), expresses his thanksgiving to God for his relation to the Gospel (vv. 12-17), and renews the charge with special thought of its recipient.

1. The Charge to Timothy to Preserve the Purity of the Gospel, vv. 3-11

Paul at once launches into the purpose of his writing. Timothy is urged to carry out the charge given to him at Ephesus when Paul left for Macedonia. His first task is to deal with the false teachers perverting the Gospel. He details the nature of the charge given to Timothy (vv. 3, 4), states the aim of the Gospel charge (v. 5), and sets forth the reasons necessitating the task laid upon him (vv. 6-11).

a. The nature of the charge, vv. 3, 4. These verses give us the historical setting and occasion for the letter. In delineating the nature of the charge Paul indicates the circumstances for its impartation (v. 3a) as well as its contents (vv. 3b, 4).

27

1) The impartation of the charge, v. 3a. "As I exhorted thee to tarry at Ephesus, when I was going into Macedonia." These words clearly imply that Paul and Timothy had been together at Ephesus and that when Paul left for Macedonia Timothy was urged to remain to carry out the task assigned to him. These historical references to Paul's movements cannot be fitted into the Acts story. On the second missionary journey Paul touched at Ephesus but from there he left for Palestine and not Macedonia. On the third missionary journey Timothy was with him at Ephesus and from there Paul left for Macedonia, but then Timothy accompanied him into Macedonia. It is evident that this Epistle belongs to the time following Paul's first imprisonment at Rome.

Apparently upon his release at Rome, Paul sailed for Ephesus, visited Colossae as he had promised Philemon (v. 22), and returned to Ephesus, where he met Timothy coming from Philippi. A survey of the situation in and around Ephesus revealed the need to check the false teachers there. Paul urged Timothy to remain to deal with the situation while he went to Macedonia in accord with his promise to visit the Philippians (Phil. 2:24). Paul turned the work over to Timothy as his representative.

Paul begins with "as" but does not write the corresponding "so." The construction is left incomplete, but the completing thought is easily supplied. This our translations do in the italicized words at the end of verse 4. The words "so do I now," supplied in the American Standard Version, are less forceful than the "so do" in the King James. Paul was more concerned that Timothy charge the false teachers than that he should merely tarry at Ephesus. That Paul had some such conclusion in mind is obvious, but the expression of it was "lost in the abundance of the thoughts that streamed in on him" (Huther). Horton remarks, "This eager breathlessness of a writer who is too absorbed in the matter to remember the grammar is a mark of Paul's style." It is characteristically Pauline but a matter which a forger could hardly duplicate.

Paul reminds Timothy of a previous exhortation given him. "As I exhorted thee." It implies that they had discussed the matter and that the charge had been orally given. In this letter "Paul repeats in writing what he had orally outlined for Timothy, both in order that Timothy might have it black on white, and that he might present it as written evidence to those who objected to Timothy's activities" (Lenski). The verb translated "exhorted" may imply that Timothy was reluctant to accept the responsibility. Paul felt that Timothy, with his experience from years of association with him, could well take care of the matter, so urged him "to continue on" at Ephesus while he went to Macedonia.

2) The contents of the charge, vv. 3b, 4. The task of Timothy was to check and suppress the strange teaching being propagated in the territory. "That thou mightest charge certain men." The term "charge" is the regular word for "an order" passed along the line and implies authority. As Paul's representative, he is to use that authority in dealing with these "certain men." Paul does not name them but refers to them as "certain ones."

These men are to be charged "not to teach a different doctrine." These words translate a negative and a present infinitive in the original. The construction implies that they are now doing it but that they must stop. The word *heteros* in the compound infinitive means "another of a different kind." These men were mingling strange and incongruous elements with their teaching of the Gospel. Because of their irrelevance and variance from the Gospel these elements might easily become hostile to it. By mingling with it elements that were foreign to its essential nature they were in reality changing the whole character of the Christian teaching. Doctrine inconsistent with the nature of the Gospel becomes false doctrine. Such teachings must be resisted. The apostolic teaching was the norm by which all teaching must be measured.

Scholars are not agreed as to the source and precise nature of these divergent elements which these men were introducing. Some see in this teaching the influence of Gentile gnostic philosophy with its speculative views of religious beliefs and practices. Such incipient gnostic elements did circulate in Asia during the latter half of the first century and may have been present here. But that the false teaching combatted in the Pastorals had already become Gnostic in character is doubtful. The Jewish character of the teaching here denounced is obvious. These men claimed to be "teachers of the law" (v. 7). They were occupied with "fables and endless genealogies" (v. 4). In 4:7 Paul characterizes the teaching as "profane and old wives' fables," and in Titus 1:14 these fables are stamped as being Jewish. By their introduction of and preoccupation with matters incongruous with the Gospel they corrupted it. Lilley characterizes them thus:

> Some tried to dazzle the minds of the people with matters that lay outside the sphere of revelation altogether. Others did indeed handle a Biblical theme, but in their ignorance and presumption were unable to expound it in its true relations and proportions. The one class took up fables and genealogies (v. 4): the other professed to teach the Mosaic law (v. 6).

These men Timothy is to charge "not to give heed to fables and endless genealogies." The word "to give heed to" means not merely to give attention to but to attach oneself to, to adhere to. The tense shows that they were doing this but must stop it. With the words "fables and endless genealogies," apparently two phases of the same aberration, Paul gives a more precise statement of the teaching. In New Testament usage the word translated "fables," from which we get our word "myth," means an invention, a fiction, a falsehood; it denotes something without historical reality. They were fanciful tales such as abound in the rabbinical writings. They were apparently bound up with their fictitious amplifications of the Old Testament genealogies. These genealogies were expanded, the names of wives invented, additional stories woven into them, and given wild allegorical interpretations. Paul calls them "endless" because these inventions led to no certain conclusions.

Such things ("which"—literally, "things of this character") are to be avoided because of what they do and what they fail to do. Their positive effect is to "minister questionings." Occupation with them furnishes occasion for arguments and disputes.

The negative reason for avoiding them is that they do not further "a dispensation of God which is in faith." They are not practical. By being occupied with them the Gospel is relegated to the rear and the saving purpose of God is not furthered.

The reading in the King James Version, "godly edifying" rests on a very inferior reading. The reading of the American Standard Version, following the preponderance of manuscript evidence (*oikonomian theou*), is more difficult. The expression "dispensation of God" has been differently understood. If taken objectively it means God's method or plan of administering salvation to the world. These fables and genealogies do not help that work of grace which God is carrying on but rather hinder it. It seems better to interpret it subjectively as denoting "the work of man as a steward of God." Teachers of the Gospel are stewards of God, entrusted with the duty of administering God's grace and salvation to mankind through a clear proclamation of the Gospel. The added phrase, "which is in faith," means that this trust committed to God's stewards is exercised in the sphere of faith. The teaching of these men did not further saving faith since they dealt with their pet fancies and speculations rather than the Word of God.

b. The aim of the charge, v. 5. "But the aim of the charge is love." The translation "the commandment" in the King James

Version must not mislead us to think that Paul is referring to the Mosaic law or part thereof. It is the noun form of the verb "charge" in verse 3. The charge is not merely Paul's charge to Timothy but rather the charge which Timothy is to give to the false teachers. The "but" introduces the contrast between Timothy's message and that of these pretended "law-teachers." Their teaching produced strife and contention, but the charge of Timothy has as its aim the production of true and pure love. It was such love that prompted Paul to give the charge to Timothy and this charge is aimed at producing such love in the hearts of these deluded teachers. Their sterile occupation with their fables and genealogies blocks its development. The aim of Gospel ministry is the production of love.

The ultimate source of this love is the love of God poured out in our hearts through the Holy Spirit (Rom. 5:5). It is implanted on the condition of faith, but the soil in which it grows is described as being "out of a pure heart and a good conscience and faith unfeigned." The one preposition with the three nouns unites them as a unit. "A pure heart" is a heart made pure in affection and single in purpose by faith. It is enabled to discern the presence and love of God. The "heart" in Scripture denotes the inward center of human life as the seat of spiritual emotions and desires. The word "conscience" quite literally means "knowing with" and "represents the self sitting in judgment on self; it stands for the self-conscious and rational element in the man" (Bernard). A "good conscience" is one that has been freed from the guilt of sin by the application of Christ's blood and is conscious of cherishing no impure, wicked motives. Faith is "unfeigned" or "unhypocritical" when it is not a mere lip-faith, mere pretense, but the sincere trust and confidence of the heart. "An unclean heart cannot have a conscience that is good and a faith that is unhypocritical" (Lenski). When the whole moral and spiritual nature is thus purified by the Gospel it becomes a fertile soil that bears an abundant harvest of love. But their occupation with their fables and genealogies and their pretensions as interpreters of the law choked the harvest in the lives of these men.

c. The reason for the charge, vv. 6-11. The reason necessitating the charge Paul views from the standpoint of the failure of the false teachers themselves (vv. 6, 7) as well as from the viewpoint of the truth concerning the law itself (vv. 8-11)

1) The failure of the false teachers, vv. 6, 7. Their failure lies both in the departure involved in their lives and the impure motive behind their teaching. Paul continues with a relative clause where in English we would have begun with a new sentence. "From which things" refers to those mentioned in verse 5. The failure of these teachers, to whom he again refers by the indefinite "some," lay in the sad fact that they have departed from the "pure heart and conscience good and faith unhypocritical" at which the Gospel aimed. The fact about them is that they "having swerved have turned aside." "Having swerved" is literally "having missed the mark" and graphically sets forth the change of aim which has come into their spiritual career. They once professed to follow the Gospel aim, but there came a day when they swerved away from it and "turned aside" on a different path. So instead of reaching the true goal, they turned off to "vain talking." The word translated "vain" is *mataios* which means vain in the sense that it does not lead to the goal; it is futile and ineffectual for its intended purpose. There was some content in what these teachers said, but it contributed nothing to the furtherance of the Christian life. Their vain talking, arising out of their occupation with their fables and genealogies and their views of the law, was antagonistic to evangelical results. The experience of these men is instructive. It was their failure in the moral realm which led to their perversion of the Gospel. "The heart is the real source of error in religion. Sin blinds the spiritual perceptions and perverts the spiritual

judgment. All false religious tendencies originate in a perverted heart" (Harvey).

In verse 7 Paul indicates their motive—"desiring to be teachers of the law." The word "desiring" implies that it was their continuing wish or resolution. They aimed at being professional interpreters of the law. They coveted the honor and respect which was paid to the acknowledged teachers of the Mosaic law. That they wanted to be "teachers of the law" plainly shows that the false teaching had its roots in Judaism, but it does not thereby follow that these were the Judaizers whom Paul combatted in Galatians. Their desire to be exponents of the law was good but they failed because they lacked the necessary qualifications. "Though they understand neither what they say, nor whereof they confidently affirm." They were insincere and misguided and did not speak from inner conviction but made up for its lack by the strenuousness with which they set forth their assertions. They failed clearly to apprehend the real significance of the law in its relations to the Gospel, nor did they truly understand the implications of the subjects concerning which they dogmatized.

2) The true knowledge concerning the law, vv. 8-11. Having exposed the failure of the false teachers to understand the use of the law, Paul now sets forth the truth concerning it. He thus shows his own understanding on the matter and guards against any suspicion that he is against the law. He presents the true nature of the law (v. 8), indicates its purpose (vv. 9, 10), and proclaims the harmony of a proper view of the law with the Gospel (v. 11).

a) The nature of the law, v. 8. His view is based upon knowledge—"but we know." "The Apostle places the declaration of his knowledge, which he has learned in the school of the Holy Ghost, against the arrogant view of the false Gnosis" (Van Oosterzee). The truth is that "the law is good." It is in accord with divine holiness, truth, and justice. (See Paul's elaboration in Rom. 7:12-16). But there is one condition, "if a man use it lawfully." By "lawfully" he means not that which the law permits but that it must be used according to its original spirit and intention. "The law itself, because it is law, dictates its lawful use and condemns every abuse as unlawful" (Lenski).

b) The purpose of the law, vv. 9, 10. The purpose of the law is considered both negatively (v. 9a) and positively (vv. 9b, 10). He points out that the law is not intended for a righteous man but for sinners. In their ignorance the false teachers reversed these facts. He passes from their ignorance to true knowledge by saying "but knowing this," thus appealing to general knowledge.

True knowledge recognizes, negatively, that "law is not made for a righteous man." "Law" is without the article and goes beyond the Mosaic law to law as such. Some hold that by "a righteous man" Paul simply means a morally upright man as contrasted to the lawless man. But in the light of verse 11, which sets the whole sentence in the light of Gospel doctrine, it seems necessary to view it here in the Christian sense, a man who has been declared righteous through faith in Christ. The liberation of the Christian from the law, either for justification or as a rule of life, is one of the cardinal principles in the teaching of Paul. The law reveals sin and condemns the sinner and shows him his need of the Saviour. By the new birth he passes out from under its domination. Having been welcomed into the gracious presence of God and filled with the spirit of righteousness, the law has no hold on the righteous man. "He is rather occupied with it as a revelation of the divine holiness, and finds in its spiritual breadth a means of humbling his heart, and so leading him to fall back on the saving power of that righteousness of God which is revealed in the Gospel from faith to faith" (Lilley). All this the false teachers failed to see.

Positively, Paul asserts that the law was enacted for sinners. "A righteous man" is in the singular, thus individualizing, but "all the wicked are named in plurals, for they are all an abominable mass" (Lenski). The list of sinners which follows is characteristically Pauline. It may be viewed as falling into two groups. (1) *Sinners as arrayed against God.* They are named in three pairs, apparently all condemned by the first table of the law. First he names "the lawless and unruly." "The lawless" refuse to recognize law, while the "unruly" refuse to be subject to law. They mean to act as they please, thus putting self before God. They are characterized by *disobedience.* The second pair are "the ungodly and sinners." "The ungodly" are people without inner reverence for God, who willfully ignore God and His commands. They are not necessarily professed atheists, but all who disregard God and His will for their lives. "Sinners" are those who in nature and action are opposed to God. *Irreverence* characterizes this pair. The third pair, "the unholy and profane," depicts people who are characterized by *impurity.* They are impure in life and irreverent toward that which is sacred. The word "profane" comes from a word meaning a "threshold," hence that which is trodden. The profane are those "who walk over everything and make it as common as dirt" (Lenski). (2) *Sinners as arrayed against society.* The first three pairs represented states of mind; what follows are examples of violations of specific commands. The first is again a pair—"Murderers of fathers and murderers of mothers." The Greek for each is a compound word which may have the wider sense of "father-smiters and mother-smiters." This is apparently in the writer's mind. They are "so lost to all natural affection and reverence that they will even strike their own parents" (Brown). For this extreme violation of the fifth commandment the law ordered the death penalty (Exod. 21:15). "Manslayers," or murderers, violate the sixth commandment. It is the supreme manifestation of human hate and was to be punished by death (Num. 35:16). The next two, "fornicators" and "abusers of themselves with men" relate to the most repulsive forms of the violation of the seventh commandment. The first refers to unchastity toward the female, the other toward the male sex. The latter, one word in the Greek, means "one who lies with a male as with a female, a Sodomite, a pederast." They are the modern "homosexuals." "Menstealers" are the kidnapers. The crime of stealing children to be sold into slavery was common in Paul's day. It is the worst form of thieving and is a violation of the eighth commandment. "Liars" and "false swearers" are guilty of bearing false witness, forbidden in the ninth commandment.

The apostle breaks off his list by saying, "if there be any other thing contrary to the sound doctrine." The form of the condition lets us understand that there are indeed other forms and shapes of unrighteousness. Only overt acts, and those the worst examples, of which the law can take cognizance, are listed, hence the tenth commandment, which deals with the inner desire, is not illustrated. The law deals with all such things as are "contrary to the sound doctrine." The word translated "doctrine" occurs fifteen times in the Pastorals and only four times elsewhere. It may mean either the act of teaching (as in Rom. 12:7; I Tim. 4:13; 5:17; Titus 2:7), or that which is taught, the body of doctrine. The latter seems clearly to be the meaning here. The expression "sound doctrine" (here, II Tim. 4:3; Titus 1:9; 2:1) has reference not to its correctness or accuracy but rather describes its nature as healthy and wholesome. It carries an implied contrast to the diseased teaching of the ignorant law-teachers, to partake of which is to make one sick (6:4). But the Gospel teaching is healthy and is productive of spiritual health.

c) The harmony of this view with the Gospel, v. 11. Verse 11 cannot appropriately be attached to anything in the preceding verse. In typical Pauline fashion, it modifies and brings to a conclusion everything said after verse 8. The view of the law which he has presented is not founded on his own private opinion but is in full accord with the Gospel, which he describes as "the gospel of the blessed God." It is not simply the "glorious gospel" as in the King James. It means the Gospel which manifests the glory of God, since it is the highest revelation of His nature and attributes. It sets forth and proclaims God's glory.

Although it is common to the rest of the New Testament, only here and in 6:15 is this word "blessed" (*makarios*) applied to God; elsewhere the word is *eulogētos*, meaning "blessed or praised" and denoting the worship of the creature. This word means "blessed or happy." God is not only the object of His creature's praise, but as "blessed" (*makarios*) has in Himself the fullness of bliss.

This reference to the Gospel leads Paul to conclude the paragraph with a statement of his relation to it. "Which was committed to me," or more literally, "with which I, even I, was entrusted." Paul was keenly conscious that his position as a commissioned messenger of the Gospel was not due to any personal merit or choice; it was a divine trust to him. This concluding reference to that fact is appropriate in a passage where he is opposing his own teaching to that of the false teachers and vouches for its wholesomeness.

2. The Apostle's Thanksgiving for His Relation to the Gospel, vv. 12-17

This outburst of praise for the mercy shown him and his appointment to God's service is an elaboration of the concluding expression of the preceding paragraph. "The glory of the message of Christianity shone ever so brightly before him that he could hardly think of his position as a divinely appointed herald of it, as compared with his former attitude of antagonism (v. 13), without magnifying anew the mercy shown to him (vv. 14-17)" (Lilley).

This development of his relation to the Gospel is characteristic of Paul (cf. I Cor. 15:9-10; Eph. 3:8; Col. 1:23-25). But this is not simply an unrelated digression, the writer going off on a tangent at a favorite thought. Amid apparent digression he is building up his case for the Gospel against the false teachers. His own case is the best illustration of the true relation of the law to the Gospel and clearly shows how deep is the contrast between the Gospel and the speculations of these false teachers. His soul is stirred to its depth as he thinks of the folly of these men and their perversion of the Gospel which has done so much for him. Failure on his part to oppose them would have been a practical denial of his own experience and apostolic commission. This personal testimony will strengthen Timothy in the execution of his task in regard to these false teachers.

In this paragraph Paul expresses his gratitude for his Gospel call (v. 12), describes the dark past of the one divinely appointed to service (v. 13a), gives an explanation of the appointment (vv. 13b-16), and concludes with a grand doxology of praise to God (v. 17).

a. The thanksgiving for his appointment to God's service, v. 12. As Paul's thoughts turn to his own experience gratitude fills his soul. "I thank him that enabled me, even Christ Jesus our Lord." The words "I thank" literally are "gratitude I am having." It is not a passing expression of thanks but the revelation of a constant attitude of gratitude, as the present tense shows. His gratitude is directed toward Him "that enabled me," or "put strength within me." He is referring to that new motivation and spiritual dynamic which was imparted to him by the divine forgiveness. The aorist tense points back to a definite time when he received this impartation of strength. The One who equipped him for service in the power of the Holy Spirit was "Christ Jesus our Lord." His use of "our" indicates that the Lord who thus dealt with him is likewise Timothy's Lord and Enabler.

The reason for his gratitude is "that he counted me faithful, appointing me to his service." "Faithful" does not mean "believing" but "trustworthy." Not skill or knowledge but faithfulness is the first qualification for a minister of Christ (I Cor. 4:2). The evidence of the divine regard of him as faithful was his appointment to service. This quality of faithfulness, which seems to be the reason why the Lord chose him for this great work, Paul in I Corinthians 7:27 refers to as a gift of grace which he had obtained from the Lord. Paul here does not speak of his appointment to "apostleship" but rather to "service." The rendering of the King James Version, "the ministry," is too specific and has developed a specialized connotation today as relating to the ordained clergy. The word rather means service of any kind with the thought of carrying out the commands of another. The official status of the one serving is not involved.

b. The description of the one appointed, v. 13a. It was the remembrance of his career as an opponent of Christianity that enhanced Paul's gratitude for his appointment. "Though I was before a blasphemer, and a persecutor, and injurious." In the original the order of this triad forms an ascending scale of sin. He has been a "blasphemer" of the name of the Lord Jesus in the truest sense of that terrible word. He repudiated Christ's Messianic claims and stamped Him as an impostor. His sin was double-dyed because he himself thus spoke against the Lord and tried to force others to do the same (Acts 26:11). As a fiery "persecutor" he vigorously pursued the Lord's people as one chases an animal (Acts 22:4), and that even unto foreign cities. The translation "injurious" forms an anticlimax in the English. The original word (*hubristēn*) means one whose insolence and contempt of others break forth in wanton and outrageous acts. Brown says, "If the term could be allowed, 'a bully'—one who not only ill-treats others but does so with the insolence of superior strength." The climax is preserved if we translated it "a doer of outrage." Such is Paul's straightforward judgment upon his former conduct.

c. The explanation for the appointment, vv. 13b-16. The grace of Christ stands in striking contrast to his own shameful conduct. It alone explains his appointment to the service of the Gospel. This appointment he sees as due to the outpouring of God's grace on him (vv. 13b, 14) as well as to God's purpose of making him an example of His grace to others (vv. 15, 16).

1) The outpouring of God's grace on him, vv. 13b, 14. "Howbeit I obtained mercy." That mercy which he wished Timothy in the salutation he has himself experienced. The verb in the Greek is passive and quite literally would be "I was mercied." The mercy bestowed was not given in response to any act of his own; he was the undeserving object of divine pitying love. God could act in mercy toward him "because I did it ignorantly in unbelief." Paul is not seeking to mitigate his guilt. His ignorance did not excuse him. Ignorance is itself part of the result of sin and is itself sinful. But he had not deliberately acted against better convictions, stubbornly hardened his heart, or willfully resisted the Holy Spirit. He had acted in blind unreasoning prejudice, mistakenly thinking he was thereby doing God a service (Acts 26:9). It had not set him beyond the pale of divine compassion. When his ignorance was shattered on the Damascus road by a mighty burst of enlightenment he was no longer an unbeliever.

Lest his reference to his ignorance seem to weaken the grace of God, he now sets it forth in all its riches. "And the grace of our Lord abounded exceedingly." "Grace," the undeserved favor of God, "abounded," literally, "overflowed" its wonted channels, covering all of his sins. The fullness of the flood of grace poured out on him far surpassed that shown to ordinary sinners.

That this grace was successful in Paul's case is indicated in the words "with faith and love which is in Christ Jesus." (Scholars are generally agreed that the "which" refers both to faith and love.) The "faith and love," standing in contrast to the unbelief and hatred of his previous life, speak of the change which God's grace wrought within him. They are "the subjective concomitants and results of the flood of grace" (Harvey). "In Christ Jesus" is the sphere in which they live, move, and have their being.

2) The purpose of God's grace through him, vv. 15, 16. Paul was keenly conscious that God in thus pouring out His grace on him had a larger purpose in doing so. The salvation of Paul was indicative of God's saving purpose for all sinners and was divinely intended to be an example for others who would believe in Christ.

Paul first sets forth God's saving purpose for mankind. "Faithful is the saying." This formula is peculiar to the Pastoral Epistles (here; 3:1; 4:9; Titus 3:8; II Tim. 2:11). At least here and in II Timothy 2:11 the words seem definitely to introduce the quotation of some pithy utterance of evangelical truth current in Christian circles. "Faithful" again means trustworthy and indicates that Paul evaluates the saying as a maxim on which full reliance may be placed. "And worthy of all acceptation." (Only here and in 4:9 is this phrase added.) "Acceptation" carries the idea of approval and welcome. "All" acceptation means that it is worthy to be accepted "in every way, without reservations, without hesitation, without the least doubt" (Lenski). Others interpret it in the sense of "universal" acceptance.

This faithful saying is "that Christ Jesus came into the world to save sinners." It summarizes the essence of the Christian message, stressing the purpose of the First Advent. The "world" here means the physical world into which Christ came at the incarnation. It has often been pointed out that "came" implies the pre-existence of Him who came into the world. The object of the incarnation was "to save sinners." The emphasis is on "sinners." The nature of the sinners Christ came to save has been shown in verses 9 and 10.

The saving purpose of Christ concerning sinners generally included Paul. "Of whom I am chief." He says not "was" but "am" and even adds the emphatic personal pronoun "I" (*egō*). "Chief" is literally "first," not in time but in rank. He considers himself the foremost of sinners. It is a striking confession of his own sense of sinfulness, and that at the end of his illustrious life. Such language is not to be discounted as mere rhetoric. It is a straightforward statement of his inner conviction. Brown well remarks:

> The fact is that it is always the characteristic of a true saint to feel himself a real sinner. The air in a room seems to be clear, but when it is penetrated by the sunlight it is seen to be full of dust and other impurities: and so as men draw nearer to God, and are penetrated by the light of God (I John 1:5), they see more clearly their own infirmities, and begin to feel for sin something of the hatred which God feels for it.

After acknowledging himself as the foremost of sinners, Paul gives the reason why *he* received mercy from the Lord. "For this cause I obtained mercy, that in me as chief might Jesus Christ show forth all his longsuffering." The career and conversion of Paul afforded Christ the occasion for an exemplification of "all his longsuffering." His case as a sinner drew out to its utmost extent "the whole of His longsuffering." "Longsuffering" is the divine attribute of God whereby He does not at once punish the sinner but forbears long under provocation and gives him opportunity to repent. "In the pardon of one less wicked than Paul, this grace could not have shown its full glory; but in him, 'the chief,' is revealed 'all his longsuffering,' so that Paul's conversion appears a very marvel of the love of Jesus Christ for sinners" (Van Oosterzee).

Thus Paul came to see in his conversion a larger purpose of God. It was "for an ensample of them that should thereafter believe on him unto eternal life." His conversion had world significance. "Paul stood before the eyes of all after generations as a witness to the power, the grace, and the love of the Lord;

so that the greatest of sinners need not doubt that grace" (Van Oosterzee). God had made him an "ensample" or "outline sketch" for the salvation of others. In his case "God has as it were sketched His own character in outline, and though many touches are required to complete the picture, they must all fall within—they cannot surpass—the extreme instance of His pardoning love which He has shown in this case" (Brown).

The saved are described as those that "believe on him unto eternal life." They continue to have their faith centered on Christ Jesus. The expression "on him" (*epi* with the locative) pictures the faith as resting on Christ as the sure and abiding foundation. The goal of that faith is "unto eternal life." It is imparted to us now but finds its consummation in eternity. It is not merely unending life but "connotes also life that is spiritual and therefore most real, life that is instinct with the energy and buoyancy and gladness of heaven, the life that is in the Son of God, yea, in God himself" (Lilley).

d. The doxology of praise, v. 17. Paul's thanksgiving turns into direct praise and worship. "Even in pastoral correspondence, the heart of this theologian beats with the pulse of the psalmist" (Lilley).

He addresses God as "the King eternal," literally, "the King of the ages." This title, used only here in the New Testament, pictures Him as the sovereign Controller and Dispenser of all the succeeding ages and all in them. Three co-ordinated epithets, modifying "God," are named. He is "immortal, invisible, the only God." "Immortal" is literally "incorruptible, imperishable," and speaks of His unchanging nature in contrast to the beings of earth. "Invisible" sets Him in contrast to the visible creation. He is the "only God" or "sole God," for there is none other beside Him. (The word "wise" in the King James Version is omitted by most ancient manuscripts and is perhaps inserted here from Rom. 16:27.) To Him Paul ascribes "honor and glory." And the duration of the worship ascribed to Him is "forever and ever." Literally it is "unto the ages of the ages." It is the strongest term in the Greek for eternity. The infinite future is viewed as a series of ages of ages stretching endlessly onward. Surely every believing heart that likewise has experienced the grace of Christ joins in with the apostle's "Amen."

3. The Renewal of the Charge to Timothy, 1:18-20

In this closing paragraph of the first division Paul again turns directly to Timothy with his charge. He points out the duty of Timothy (vv. 18, 19a) and by contrast speaks of the shipwreck of certain men (vv. 19b, 20).

a. The duty of Timothy, vv. 18, 19a. There is a solemnity about Paul's address to Timothy and his invoking of the memories of the prophecies which led to Timothy. "This charge I commit unto thee, my child Timothy, according to the prophecies which led the way to thee." "This charge" is the one named by the verb in verse 3 and the noun in verse 5. The verb translated "commit" means "to place alongside of, to set before," and in the middle voice, as here, means "to deposit, to intrust" as with a treasure that must be guarded. The terms of the direct address indicate a tender concern for Timothy.

The charge he describes as being "according to the prophecies which led the way to thee." The charge to Timothy to war the good warfare is "according to" or "in harmony with" those prophecies. The reference doubtless takes us into the assembly of the believers where the Holy Spirit, speaking through His prophets, singled out Timothy for special duty. These prophecies, previous to his ordination, marked him out for his office and sanctioned the laying on of hands. Thus in Acts 13 the Spirit's message, marking out Barnabas and Saul, came before they were publicly set aside for the work. So doubtless it was also in the case of Timothy.

The memory of these prophecies from the Lord are to strengthen Timothy in the performance of his duty, namely, "that by them thou mayest war the good warfare." He must continue (present tense) to "war the good warfare." This is the personal aspect of Timothy's duty at Ephesus. The military figure has reference not to a single battle but to the whole campaign. Paul, that doughty veteran in spiritual conflict, well knew that the Christian life is a continuing warfare under the banner of the King of kings. But here the special reference is to Timothy's task of contending with the false teachers.

In his campaigning Timothy must possess the subjective conditions for victory, "holding faith and a good conscience." He must continue to hold to, and not renounce, "faith and a good conscience." "In the conflict which we wage outwardly against the enemy, our chief concern is with the inner state and disposition of the heart" (Van Oosterzee). The Christian leader must personally possess the spiritual qualities he would enforce (cf. v. 5).

b. The shipwreck of certain men, vv. 19b, 20. Paul stresses the value of these moral and spiritual elements by reminding Timothy of "some" or "certain ones" who have made a failure of their warfare.—"Which some having thrust from them made shipwreck concerning the faith." "Which" has reference to "a good conscience." These false teachers treated the matter of maintaining their spiritual integrity as a minor matter as they played fast and loose with the Scriptures. When their conscience goaded them they "thrust" from them their good conscience. The word implies the violence of the act required. The result was that they "made shipwreck concerning the faith." "The faith" may mean that their own personal faith was wrecked. "The Christian teacher who does not practice what he preaches will find his faith fail him" (Lock). But more probably "the faith" is objective and means the true doctrine of the Gospel. "The yielding to sin dulls the perception of truth, and opens the way for the influx of error" (Harvey). In reality both things actually occur. "Disaster falls alike on 'faith' and 'the faith,' when a good conscience is rejected, or rather ejected" (Pope). Paul switches from the picture of a military campaign to that of a shipwreck. The picture of a shipwreck implies severe and unrecoverable loss.

These "certain ones" seem to be the worst representatives of the false teachers mentioned in verses 3, 6, 7. Paul names two individuals with whom he himself has dealt. "Of whom is Hymenaeus and Alexander; whom I delivered unto Satan." Hymenaeus seems to be identical with the false teacher mentioned in II Timothy 2:17, 18. Since Alexander was a common name it is precarious to identify him with either "Alexander the coppersmith" mentioned in II Timothy 4:14, or the Alexander mentioned in Acts 19:33.

These men Paul says, "I delivered unto Satan." The aorist refers to a past act. This difficult statement has caused much discussion. What is implied by that fearful term "delivered unto Satan"? It is generally understood as meaning "an act of excommunication, by which they were placed outside of the visible kingdom of God and, so to speak, replaced within the realm of Satan. . . . This general representation of Scripture, that outside of the visible kingdom of God on earth is the kingdom of Satan, is here probably the underlying conception" (Harvey). In the light of I Corinthians 5:5 it seems also to include the judicial infliction of bodily sickness or calamity by apostolic authority. That the expression includes more than simple exclusion from the fellowship of the church is plain.

Paul's statement shows that he has not finally abandoned them. "That they might be taught not to blaspheme" reveals that the discipline was not merely punitive but remedial in its intention. The intention was that thereby they might be "taught" or "disciplined" so as to be led to repentance. The word "blaspheme" shows that these men had arrived at a point where they were actually blaspheming (present tense) the truths of God in order to make way for and establish their fables and misrepresentations of the law. Paul hopes that the disciplinary measures taken against them may lead them to stop their offenses. "Even Satan's power in dealing with the outer man, and perhaps in the infliction of anguish of mind, may be used under the hand of God to bring down the haughty spirit and make past blasphemy to be seen in all its offensive pride and opposition to God" (Kelly).

II. THE INSTRUCTIONS CONCERNING CHURCH ORDER, 2:1-3:16

CHAPTERS 2 and 3 constitute the second main division of the Epistle and unfold the duty of Timothy in relation to the churches. The opening "therefore" is transitional and takes us from the general charge in 1:18 to the elaboration of specific duties. The division falls into three parts. Paul sets forth regulations concerning public worship (2:1-15), discusses the qualifications of church officers (3:1-13), and concludes with a personal word to Timothy in view of Christian truth (3:14-16).

1. The Regulations Concerning Public Worship, 2:1-15

This classic passage we may divide into three parts. In it Paul presents the duty of public prayer (vv. 1-7), offers instructions concerning the manner of public prayer (vv. 8-10), and concludes with instructions concerning the position of women in public worship (vv. 11-15).

a. The duty of public prayer, vv. 1-7. The word here rendered "exhort" is translated "beseech" in Romans 12:1. In such connections it carries the meaning "to beg, entreat, urge." What follows is not presented as a command but as an appeal to their conscience and their love to do what is asked of them. The practice of prayer cannot be forced by an outward command but must be prompted by an inner conviction of its need. It is better

in the words "first of all" to the opening verb "exhort"
...to what follows, as in the King James Version. The words
...ark "not priority of time, but of dignity" (Ellicott). He will
give the matter of prayer the first place in his treatment of church
affairs. The paragraph presents the nature (1a), scope (1b-2a),
result (2b), and reasons for (3-7) public prayer in the congregations.

1) The nature of public prayer, v. 1a. The apostle employs
four words to indicate the different elements in the public prayers
offered in the church. "Supplications, prayers, intercessions,
thanksgivings." These four words indicate the different elements which are to enter into the public prayers of the church.
(1) "Supplications" is a general word meaning a request or a
petition and was used of petitions addressed both to men and
God. Coming from a verb meaning "to lack," it signifies prayer
which springs from a sense of need. A conscious sense of need
is essential to all effective praying. (2) "Prayers" is distinctly a
religious term in that it was used only of prayer to God. Although unrestricted as to its contents, it carries the thought of
reverence in prayer. In public prayer irreverence in manner or
content is inexcusable. Heartfelt reverence in public prayer is
often sadly lacking. (3) "Intercessions," occurring only here
and in 4:5 in the New Testament, suggests the thought of confidence in prayer. It does not have the limitation of being *for
others,* as implied in our English term. It was used for a petition
of any kind to a superior. It speaks of personal and confiding
intercourse with God on the part of one qualified to approach
Him. A life lived in fellowship with God gives confidence in
prayer. (4) The three previous words indicate the character of
the praying while the word "thanksgivings" points out the
spirit in which our prayers are to be offered. It is the spirit of
gratitude for blessings already received and those yet to be received. It is the complement of all true prayer.

Prayer in all of these aspects the apostle urges upon the

churches as a standing duty. The tense (present) of the word "be made" shows that this is to be the habitual, repeated practice of the congregation at its public services. The failure of the church to pray in accordance with this exhortation is one of its great sins today.

2) The scope of public prayer, vv. 1b, 2a. The praying of the church is to be universal in its scope—"for all men." How far this transcends the scope of the praying ordinarily heard! It is a wholesome corrective against the narrowing tendency of church institutions and services. As adherents of the true universal faith, believers must exercise a concern and priestly intercession for a sin-darkened world. All men are sinners and need prayer on their behalf. Lenski well remarks: "If such praying were useless, the apostle would not write what he here does write."

Because men live in national groupings, the church must also pray "for kings and all that are in high place." Prayer is to be not only world-wide but also national and patriotic. "Kings" as leaders of the nations are a special class needing such prayer. This is highly important because the type of government men live under profoundly influences their lives and affects their spiritual welfare. The prayer is not to be limited to the supreme rulers but is to include all who have dignity or elevation of public office. The attitude of these minor officials may often have a more direct bearing on the local congregation than that of the supreme rulers.

3) The result of such praying, v. 2b. "That we may lead a tranquil and quiet life in all godliness and gravity." These words indicate not the contents of the prayer but the contemplated result. Paul believed that prayer made a definite difference in national affairs and brought about conditions favorable to the furtherance of the Gospel. He contemplated the resultant conditions as enabling believers to live "a tranquil and quiet life." The former word may be considered as indicating the absence

of disturbances from without while the latter may denote the absence of inner distractions. To assert that this is a selfish prayer is to miss the point, since the blessings envisioned would benefit the entire nation. The ultimate purpose however is the salvation of souls, as verse 4 shows.

Such circumstances demand that the believer live "in all godliness and gravity." The believer's life is characterized in its twofold relationship. Godward, his life must be "in godliness," reverent and respectful, dominated by the fear of the Lord. Manward, his life must be characterized by "gravity." The meaning of the term is wider than "honesty" (King James Version) in its modern connotations. It denotes that decent and becoming deportment which commands the respect of others. "This gravity is the attitude of men who take a serious, though by no means a gloomy, view of life and its obligations" (Brown). The word "all" is to be construed with both "godliness" and "gravity" as indicating that both are to be complete in the believer. If believers were always exemplifying such character, the salvation of souls would be greatly furthered.

4) The reasons for such prayer, vv. 3-7. Paul advances some weighty considerations in support of his appeal for such praying by the local congregations. The reasons advanced constitute a logical progression of facts. Such prayer is to be engaged in, not because Paul urges it, but because of its intrinsic nature (v. 3), as well as the facts that it is in accord with God's will (v. 4), Christian doctrine (vv. 5, 6), and the nature of Paul's ministry (v. 7).

a) Its intrinsic nature, v. 3. "This is good." (The opening "for" in the King James Version rests on insufficient manuscript evidence.) The word "good" means that it is excellent in its nature and characteristics and is well-adapted to its ends. "This practice of praying for all men is a fine thing in itself; i.e., it approves itself to the moral sense of mankind" (Brown). It is good and wholesome in the spirit which it reveals and beneficial in the results that it achieves. It is quite possible to connect this with what follows and read it as one thought, that such prayer is both good and acceptable before God. It seems better, however, to take it as a separate statement of the nature of prayer.

Such prayer is further characterized as being "acceptable in the sight of God our Saviour." For the believer this is ever the chief motive for obeying this exhortation. The designation "God our Saviour" is appropriate in view of the following verse (cf. 1:1).

b) Its accord with God's will, v. 4. Such praying is motivated by the fact that it is in accord with the saving purpose of God. "Who would have all men to be saved." "All men" is emphatic by position. (Notice the accumulation of the word "all" in these verses.) It must not be so restricted as to denote merely "all classes of men" (cf. Ezek. 33:11; II Peter 3:9). God's desire for the salvation of everyone springs spontaneously from His love for a lost race. But that does not mean that all will be saved. If Paul had used the active infinitive "to save," rather than the passive, that might have been implied. That some men are not saved is not due to any inefficacy or deliberate limitation in the divine will, but is due to man's rejection of God's appointed means of salvation through faith in Christ Jesus.

God's further desire for men is that they should "come to the knowledge of the truth." This may be regarded as the means of salvation, or it may be thought of as the goal of God's saving work. The latter seems preferable. While it is true that man must have certain knowledge of the truth to be saved, there remains yet much to be learned after he is saved. Having been rescued from sin and ignorance, there follows "an advance from this first knowledge of one's true self as a sinner to the complete and perfect knowledge of the truth" (Humphreys). The compound form of the word "knowledge" (*epignōsis*) expresses a deeper and fuller knowledge which advances toward a goal. Too many Christians never advance to an experiential knowledge of the full purpose of God for them.

c) Its accord with Christian doctrine, vv. 5, 6. The universal scope of prayer as being in accord with God's desire for the salvation of the race is now grounded in the facts of Christian doctrine. These verses present a brief creed. They set forth the unity of God, the mediatorial work of Christ, and the universality of His atonement.

"For there is one God." The unity of God was central in the Hebrew revelation. It carries with it the truth that God, being one, stands in the same ultimate relation to all His creatures and that His divine purposes of love and mercy must embrace all men alike. If there were various purposes for various individuals the Godhead would be divided in its nature.

"One mediator also between God and men, *himself* man, Christ Jesus." A mediator is one who stands between two parties who are at variance in order to reconcile them. A mediator "between God and men" must have in his life features that identify him with both God and man. Christ Jesus is such a Mediator. (The mediation of saints or angels is unscriptural.) The divine aspect of His nature is here assumed but the fact of His true humanity is expressly asserted, "himself man." The word "man" is not *anēr*, "a male individual," but the racial term *anthrōpos*. "In Him all men are summed up, and so He is the representative, not of this or that man only, but of all mankind" (Bernard). The article is not used in the original. "It is not *the* man, nor *a* man, but MAN, humanity exalted to true manhood by its union with God in the person of Christ Jesus" (Harvey). Since there is "one" Mediator only it follows that He is the Mediator of all mankind, thus opening up the way to all men alike.

The appositional statement, "who gave himself a ransom for all," sets forth the act by which He realized this universal mediatorship. "Gave" speaks of a voluntary act of self-giving on His part. "His voluntary sacrifice reveals all the greatness and nobility of his love, and settles once for all the charge of injustice on the part of God, that he should have unjustly punished the innocent instead of the guilty" (Lenski). That He gave "himself" speaks of the completeness of the gift. "He gave, not his life only, but himself, in his whole personality and work, including His humiliation, suffering, and death" (Harvey). The gift was made "as a ransom for all." The statement attests the substitutionary nature of the death of Christ both by the noun and the preposition. The noun "ransom" (*antilutron*), which occurs only here in the New Testament, is a compound form made up of the substitutionary preposition *anti*, "instead of," and the word *lutron*, meaning "a ransom-price." "In this important word," says Ellicott, "the idea of a substitution of Christ in our stead cannot be ignored." This idea is further shown by the preposition "for" (*huper*) all men. Papyrus evidence conclusively proves that it was used in the substitutionary sense of "on behalf of, instead of." Hence Bernard remarks: "Both the elements represented by *anti* instead of, and *huper* on behalf of, must enter into any Scriptural theory of the Atonement." The universality of the atonement is asserted in "all." The atonement of Christ was not made for a limited number but for all men.

The words "the testimony *to be borne* in its own times" stand in apposition to the preceding sentence. The content of the apostolic testimony is that God is one and Christ, who gave Himself a ransom for all, is the one Mediator between God and men. That testimony "could be borne only when the fullness of time had come, and the Incarnation had presented a mediator for all men" (Horton). The historic work of Christ on the cross introduced the due times for the proclamation of this message.

d) Its accord with Paul's ministry, v. 7. Prayer for all men is also in accord with Paul's appointment to testify to these great

Gospel facts. The reference to the Gospel testimony again leads Paul to indicate his own relation to it (cf. 1:12). It was a divine appointment, not a self-chosen ministry. The Twelve had been appointed by Christ; he too (emphatic pronoun, "I on my part") received an appointment, and that as "a preacher and an apostle . . . a teacher of the Gentiles." The Greek word for "preacher" is "herald," one who makes a public announcement as ordered by another. The word is indicative of the nature of his work, while "apostle" denotes the authority of the worker. The abrupt and emphatic parenthesis, "I speak the truth, I lie not," is quite in accord with Paul's style (cf. Rom. 9:1; II Cor. 11:31). It may be taken to refer either to what precedes or to what follows. If to the former, it is a strong assertion of his apostolic authority in reaction to the denials and attacks of the false teachers. But since the false teachers do not appear in this context, it seems much better to take it with "a teacher of the Gentiles." This was the distinctive feature of his appointment as an apostle and accords with his emphasis upon the universality of the Gospel message. His appointment as "herald and apostle" had made him "a teacher of Gentiles." The concluding phrase "in faith and truth" indicates the element or sphere in which he discharges his office as teacher of Gentiles. He preaches with a sincere faith in the Gospel and makes a truthful presentation of the Gospel which he believes.

b. The manner of public prayer, vv. 8-10. The "therefore" is resumptive of the exhortation given in verse 1. Following his elaboration of the reasons for universal prayer, the apostle now turns to a presentation of the manner of public prayer, giving instructions both for the men (v. 8) and the women (vv. 9, 10). The opening expression "I desire" has in it the note of authority. It is a positive apostolic direction.

1) The praying of the men, v. 8. "I desire that the men pray." The word "pray" is again in the present tense and indicates that this is to be the habitual practice in the congrega-

tional worship. It includes all that was depicted by the four nouns in verse 1. "The men" (*tous andras*) points specifically to the men as distinguished from the women. The men only are to lead in public prayer. The words also imply that all the men of the congregation were desired to take part in public prayer. Public prayer was not restricted to the leaders of the church. "The time of liturgies and priests and formal reading of prayers was not yet" (Horton). These regulations were to be universally observed, "in every place," that is, in every city where believers assembled for public worship.

Moral qualifications for those leading in public prayer are set forth. The words "lifting up holy hands" describe both the bodily posture and the character of the one praying. Standing to pray with upraised hands was regarded as reverent among the Jews and was common in the early Church. "The folding together of the hands in prayer has been shown to be of Indo-Germanic origin" (Ellicott). Other postures in prayer are mentioned in the Bible. The important matter is not the bodily posture but the inner life. The one leading in prayer must have "holy hands," hands unstained with sin through employment in impure deeds. He who would lead others to the throne of God must be morally qualified to do so.

The concluding phrase "without wrath and disputing" sets forth two conditions for effectual public prayer. "Wrath" relates to the personal attitude toward others, the inner disposition of ill-will and resentment. We cannot truly pray for those with whom we are angry, nor can we be angry with those for whom we truly pray. Views are divided as to the connotation of the second word. Its basic meaning is that of wrong thoughts or deliberations of any kind, and the question is whether we are to understand it of inward disputings, that is, "doubts," as in the King James Version, or of outward disputations and arguments. The latter view, favored by papyrus usage, indicates the outward manifestation of these wrong thoughts in angry discussions, hence "disputations" in the American Standard Version. "To introduce disputes into prayer is to pray at one another instead of to God" (Horton). Unless repented of and removed, both the inner attitude and its outward manifestation disqualify one to lead in public prayer.

2) The adorning of the women, vv. 9, 10. Having indicated the part of the men in public worship, the apostle "in like manner" sets forth his desire concerning the adorning of the women. Some, by supplying the word "pray" here from verse 8, seek to find in these words permission also for the women to pray if certain conditions of decency are observed. But in view of what follows it is clear that Paul has reference not to their praying but to their decorum in the assembly. Their proper glory is to be found, not in active leadership in public worship, but in that beauty of personality which is the result of active beneficence.

The verb "adorn" means "to put in order, arrange, prepare," and it indicates that the adornment of the Christian woman should be one in which order obtains. "Say what some will about Paul, he here states that women are to dress in good taste when they prepare to attend church" (Lenski). Slovenliness in dress and appearance is unbecoming a Christian woman. Outwardly her adorning should be "in modest apparel." The word here translated "apparel" (*katastolē*) may have a wider meaning than simply dress and may denote the deportment exhibited externally whether in look, manner, or dress. The appropriate dress or deportment must be accompanied by the proper inward feeling, "with shamefastness and sobriety." The word "shamefastness" has become obsolete for the modern reader. (The reading "shamefacedness" in the King James Version is a printer's corruption of this word used in the 1611 edition.) "Modesty" gives the meaning quite well. The original denotes that self-respect which shrinks from all that is immodest and unseemly and bases respect for others on self-respect. "Sobriety" denotes "the well-balanced state of mind resulting from habitual self-restraint" (Ellicott). It is indicative of that sound judgment which should characterize the Christian woman in these matters.

The common feminine tendency to extravagant personal adornment was so strong in Paul's day that he felt it necessary to add a specific reference to it. "Not with braided hair, and gold or pearls or costly raiment." The reference is to "the custom then prevalent in fashionable life, of interweaving in the hair gold, silver, pearls, causing it to flash brilliantly in the light" (Harvey). All excesses of personal adornment which are opposed to the orderliness and simplicity of communion with God are in view in Paul's prohibition. He would exclude all that might distract the worshiper or reflect upon the spiritual dignity of the members. The caution is much needed today.

The true source of the Christian woman's adornment is that of inner character. "But (which becometh women professing godliness) through good works." The parenthesis points out that simplicity of dress is consistent with their Christian profession. Christian women may find their best and richest adornment in that beauty of character achieved through "good works." Good works react on character and create that spiritual adornment which is the real glory of the Christian woman. When she uses this as her chief adornment her apparel will be in keeping with her Christian character.

c. The position of the women in public worship, vv. 11-15. Paul proceeds to define the position of the women in public worship. From a consideration of the woman's adornment for attendance at public worship, Paul passes to a consideration of her position in the worship service. He issues a command concerning the woman (v. 11), sets forth a restriction on her activity (v. 12), and gives two reasons as a vindication of the restriction (vv. 13-15).

1) The command concerning the woman, v. 11. "Let a woman learn in quietness with all subjection." Instead of con-

tinuing with the plural, women as a class, Paul now uses the individualizing singular. Her position is to be "that of a silent learner, in manner and in act yielding subjection in all lawful respects to the authority that God has given to man as leader of worship in the assembly of the church" (Harvey). The imperative "learn" (present tense) means that instead of presuming to lead she is to have the attitude of attending to the teaching of others to learn from it what is needful for spiritual growth and advancement. "This injunction does not mean that Christian women are to surrender their mind and conscience to the dictation of men. . . . Only, their general attitude is to be that of willing listeners" (Lilley). As a learner she is to be "in quietness," not talking or seeking to instruct others. She is to be in "complete subjection" by voluntarily ranging herself under the divinely instituted headship of the man. The Gospel elevated the woman and gave her a position of spiritual equality with the man before God, but it does not remove the original position of subordination that God ordained for the woman.

2) The restriction upon the woman, v. 12. "But I permit not a woman to teach, nor to have dominion over a man." The present infinitive "to teach" denotes not a single act but a process and means that Paul does not permit a woman to assume the office of a public teacher in the congregation. The infinitive "to have dominion over" denotes one who rules over another, a master, or more strongly, an autocrat. "Man" is *anēr*, the male sex in distinction from the woman. Therein lies the point of the prohibition. For a woman to assume a position of domination over the man is inconsistent with her divinely assigned position of subordination to the man. The position of teacher or preacher in the assembly implies superiority and authority over those taught. The teacher acts as the master who is to be heard and heeded. Such a domination a woman assumes in being a public teacher in the assembly. "No woman may step into the place of the man without violating the very Word she would

try to teach to both women and men" (Lenski). The repetition of the demand "to be in quietness" brings out, by contrast, the proper position of the Christian woman.

Paul is not referring to secular instruction in the schoolroom but to the official position of the public teacher in the Christian assembly. But the New Testament as well as church history shows that women have an honorable and indispensable ministry in the church without transgressing upon the position which God has reserved to the men. Titus 2:3, 4 assigns them a teaching ministry among their own sex and the children. Priscilla was not out of place when she with her husband helped the learned Apollos to know the way of the Lord more accurately (Acts 18:26). Paul gratefully acknowledges that Euodia and Syntyche had labored with him in the Gospel but that does not warrant the inference that they preached (Phil. 4:2, 3).

3) The vindication of the restriction, vv. 13-15. Paul presents two reasons for the subordination of the woman. The insistence upon her subordination is vindicated from the order of creation (v. 13) as well as the story of the fall (vv. 14, 15).

a) The vindication from the order of creation, v. 13. "For Adam was first formed, then Eve." The Genesis story of creation shows that man was formed first, then the woman (Gen. 2:7, 20-23). They were not formed at the same time, but Eve was formed later to be his helpmate. The creative order "certainly reveals God's intent, that Eve was not to direct, rule, supervise him, that she was not to be the head, but he" (Lenski). The establishment of this relation antedates the entry of sin, thus indicating that it was God's original intention.

b) The vindication from the story of the fall, vv. 14, 15. The "and" introduces a further vindication from the story of the fall. "Adam was not beguiled, but the woman being beguiled hath fallen into transgression." Both Adam and Eve sinned, but what Adam did he did of his own choice, quite aware of the magnitude of the sin he was voluntarily committing. But Eve was completely, thoroughly deceived, as the preposition in the compound participle *exapatētheisa* indicates. (In the Genesis story only Eve pleads the excuse of being the victim of deception.) As a result of her exercise of unwarranted leadership she fell into sin and led Adam into it. "Hath fallen [perfect tense] into transgression" marks the abiding result of her act. The "transgression" was a deliberate "stepping aside," a deviation from the plain command of God. Because the woman had allowed herself to be deceived by the serpent the judgment of God was passed upon her, and in this was included the fact that her husband would rule over her (Gen. 3:16).

With verse 15 Paul "passes from Eve, the mother and prototype of the sex, to womankind generally" (Bernard). He points out the destiny which has been assigned to the woman. "She shall be saved from the results of sin and be enabled to maintain a position of influence in the Church by accepting her natural destination as a wife and mother, provided this surrender is further ratified by bringing forth the fruit of sanctified Christian character" (Lilley).

The expression, "she shall be saved through her child-bearing," does not mean that the bearing of children is the meritorious cause of her salvation. The preposition "through" here does not denote agency but accompanying circumstances. "Childbearing" denotes the proper sphere in which the woman finds the true fulfillment of her destiny. It speaks of the highest ideal of Christian womanhood. It brings out that which is noblest and best within her being. Paul's thought naturally includes the training of the children in a Christian home. It stands in opposition to the sphere of public teaching which was closed to her.

But the fulfillment of the duties of motherhood alone does not assure her salvation. "If they [i.e., the women] continue in faith and love and sanctification with sobriety." They must possess and continue in personal faith, love for God and man, and show the resultant sanctification of life. "Sanctification" includes all the graces of Christian character, but among them "sobriety" is once more (cf. 2:9) singled out as a crowning feature of Christian womanhood.

2. The Qualifications of Church Officers, 3:1-13.

From regulations concerning public worship Paul naturally passes to a consideration of the qualifications of local church officers. Timothy is to see that qualified men are placed in office. These are the established local officials; the work of Timothy does not interfere with this local organization. Paul sets forth the qualifications for a bishop (vv. 1-7) and for deacons (vv. 8-12), inserting a parenthetical sentence concerning women church workers (v. 11), and concludes with a word about the reward of faithful service (v. 13).

a. The qualifications for a bishop, vv. 1-7. Only in passing does Paul indicate the function of a bishop; the chief emphasis lies upon his moral and spiritual qualifications. The apostle points out the desirability of the office (v. 1) and delineates the qualifications for office (vv. 2-7).

1) The desirability of the office, v. 1. Some would connect the words "faithful is the saying" with the preceding section (cf. 1:15). But it seems rather to be designed to emphasize the following statement as important and worthy of confidence. "If a man seeketh the office of a bishop, he desireth a good work." The verb "seeketh" is literally "to stretch oneself out after," hence to aspire to; it does not here have a depreciatory implication. It points to an aspiration such as causes a young man to study, labor, and sacrifice in order to equip himself for leadership in the church. "The office of a bishop" is one word in the Greek (*episkopē*) and is perhaps best translated "overseership." It designates the office of the overseer or bishop by means of its

chief work, the care and oversight of the church (cf. I Peter 5:2; Acts 20:28). In the New Testament the terms "bishop" and "elder" are used interchangeably to designate the same individual, but with a difference in connotation. The term "bishop" (*episkopos*), coming from the Greek, points to the function of the officer as specifically that of having oversight; the word "elder" (*presbuteros*), derived from Jewish usage, emphasizes the personal dignity and maturity of the person holding the office. All official distinctions between the two terms, elevating the one above the other, are of postapostolic origin. The Pastoral Epistles reveal nothing of this second-century distinction.

This aspiration to overseership Paul commends and encourages by saying "he desireth a good work." Paul credits the aspirant with the noblest ideals. It is not an easy or lucrative position but is "a good work." "The adjective expresses the excellence, the noun the difficulty of the work" (Van Oosterzee). It was a difficult and often a thankless task, full of risk and danger; this might well cause a man to shrink from it. Apparently Paul felt "it necessary to dwell on the spiritual glory of such a vocation, which ought to outweigh all the counsels of worldly prudence" (Brown).

2) The qualifications for the office, vv. 2-7. The very nature and importance of the office made it necessary that only qualified men be appointed. Paul names fifteen qualifications. He marks no clear divisions in the list but the construction clearly sets off the last qualification from the preceding fourteen. For convenience we may divide the list into two groups of seven (vv. 2, 3-6), and the concluding qualification as to community standing (v. 7).

a) The first seven qualifications, v. 2. 1. "Without reproach" is a general character qualification stating that he must give no just cause for blame. The word is literally "not to be laid hold of," hence not justly open to censure or criticism. 2. "The husband of one wife" sets forth his marital qualification. Three views have been taken of this much-discussed qualification. a. That he *must be married*. This cannot be meant since Paul says "one" not "a" wife. Paul naturally assumes that he would be married, since elders were chosen from the mature men in the congregation. This requirement rules out the Roman Catholic dogma of the celibacy of the clergy. b. That he *must not remarry* if his first wife dies. This is the view prevailing in the Greek and Oriental churches. Yet this seems highly improbable in view of Paul's clear teaching concerning second marriages (I Tim. 5:14; Rom. 7:2, 3; I Cor. 7:39). Why should remarriage be such a sin that of all sexual requirements it alone should be singled out? c. That he *must not have more than one wife living* at a time. He must not be a bigamist or polygamist, or have been divorced on insufficient grounds. Both the teaching of the New Testament and the conditions prevalent in contemporary society point to this as Paul's meaning. 3 to 5. The next three, "temperate, sober-minded, orderly," relate to personal qualifications. The first word is literally "unmixed with wine, wineless." When used of persons it meant "sober." The term here doubtless has this literal significance but its connotation is wider. He is to be a man sober and fully rational, in possession of the full use of all his faculties. "Sober-minded" presents the concept of a well-balanced, properly regulated mind, a person discreet and prudent. The word "orderly," denoting order as contrasted to disorder, characterizes him as ordering well both his inner and outer life. The last two qualifications in verse 2 deal with his relations to others. 6. "Given to hospitality" means that he must be characterized by a willingness to receive into his home and care for Christian strangers. It was a matter of no small importance that the elder should be a man who loved to entertain Christian travelers as well as those who might be in flight because of persecution. 7. "Apt to teach" includes both the willingness and the skill or ability to teach. The ability to teach implies the qualification of having himself been taught. "The more a faithful teacher teaches, the more will he feel the need of acquiring more and more knowledge of the blessed truth he is to teach" (Lenski). Only here and in verse 5 is there any indication of the work of the bishop.

b) The second seven qualifications, vv. 3-6. The first three qualifications, two negative and a contrasting positive, set forth the bishop in his actions toward others. 1. The words rendered "no brawler" literally mean "not alongside of wine," and then of persons was used of one acting under the influence of too much wine. Spence remarks: "Drunkenness is scarcely alluded to here. It is rather a warning against choosing for the sacred office one given to frequently noisy banquets, where wild and imprudent words are often spoken." 2. "No striker" means that he must not be quick-tempered and ready with his fists, not given to acts of physical violence. 3. On the contrary, he is to be "gentle." He is to be mild and considerate of the feelings of others. "It is the temper which refrains from standing on one's rights and, under the inspiration of love, concedes, forbears, is no aggressive partisan" (Pope). Matthew Arnold suggestively rendered the noun "sweet reasonableness." The next two characteristics relate to his personal disposition. 4. "Not contentious" means that he must not be quarrelsome in nature or pugnacious. It does not mean that he must not contend for the truth but it must not be done in a harsh, contentious spirit. 5. "No lover of money" requires that he must be free from avarice, not mercenary, not stingy. The desire for money must not be a ruling motive in his life. 6. In verse 4 Paul gives the requirement as to his domestic relations, while verse 5 presents the reason for it. He must be a man who "ruleth well his own house," stands at the head of his household and presides over it in an excellent manner. "A minister's character is portrayed and seen to best advantage in the framework of his own family" (Lilley). His ability to preside will best be revealed in a well-ordered household where the children are in habitual subjection. "With all gravity" denotes the dignified way in which the father will secure the obedience of his children. Others take it as denoting the modesty in the bearing and deportment of the children themselves (cf. Titus 1:6). Paul undergirds the requirement by an argument from the lesser to the greater. If he shows incompetence to manage his own children, how will he be able to supervise the assembly? "Ill-trained, bad children reflect on any pastor, not merely because they are hurtful examples to the children of the members of the church, but still more because they show that the father is incompetent for his office" (Lenski). 7. "Not a novice" requires spiritual maturity of the man to be appointed as bishop. He must not be a recent convert, one newly planted in the Christian faith. To appoint such a one as bishop would be to expose him to great danger, "lest being puffed up he fall into the condemnation of the devil." The verb "puffed up" means "to raise a smoke, to emit smoke," hence metaphorically, "to blind with pride or conceit." The danger is that the novice, wrapped in smoke through his exaggerated sense of self-importance and teeming pride, would have his eyes blinded to realities. Acting thus he would "fall into the condemnation of the devil." The definite article "the devil" shows that the reference is not to some human slanderer but to the personal Devil. The expression "the condemnation of the devil" is interpreted in two ways. Some take it to mean the condemnation effected by the Devil. More probable is the view that it means the condemnation which the Devil himself incurred because of his blinding pride (cf. Isa. 14:12-15; John 8:44).

c) The qualification as to community standing, v. 7. Verses 2-6 are one sentence. With this verse Paul concludes the list and in effect returns to the first qualification of irreproachableness, but now in the light of the bishop's status in the non-Christian community. The verse implies that believers are in a minority. His character and reputation must be such that "those without" generally will give him a "good testimony," speak favorably of him as to his truthfulness, integrity, and purity.

The requirement is supported by a statement of the reason, "lest he fall into reproach and the snare of the devil." To defy public opinion in this matter would be to invite peril. For one who has an unsavory reputation in the community, to be placed by the church into a prominent place of authority would be to draw upon himself and the church the reproach of the world. The suspicion and censure thus arrayed against him and the church might easily weaken and discourage the elder. Thus weakened and disheartened he might readily fall an easy prey into some skillfully laid snare of the Devil, who is here vividly pictured as a hunter of souls. Such a fall would cause great harm to his own soul and bring terrible damage to the church. The enemy's aim has always been to destroy the leaders of the church. Hence great care must be exercised in the selection of its leaders.

b. The qualifications for deacons, vv. 8-12. From the bishop Paul abruptly passes to the deacons. They constitute the second class of officers in the apostolic churches. "Not the slightest hint is given of any class of office-bearers occupying a position intermediate to these two" (Lilley). No statement of the duties of deacons is made. The Greek term (*diakonos*) signifies, in general, one who serves, a servant in any capacity; but here it is used in a specialized sense of a class of church officers whose duty is that of an assistant ministration. Paul sets forth their personal qualifications (vv. 8, 9), gives instructions concerning the testing of deacons (v. 10), adds a parenthetical statement about women church workers (v. 11), and concludes with the mention of the domestic qualifications of deacons (v. 12).

1) The personal qualifications of the deacons, vv. 8, 9. The first qualification, "grave" or "dignified," is general and is one which every Christian should possess (see 2:2). Next he names three negative qualifications, which, if present, would disqualify the individual for the office. "Not double-tongued" points out

that he must not be guilty of saying one thing to this man and a conflicting thing to the next. "Not given to much wine" requires that they be not addicted to wine. The words "not given to" mean not only not paying attention to but not giving assent to. "The use of strong drink is entirely incompatible with a fully developed Christian character" (Lipscomb). Nor must they be "greedy of filthy lucre," that is, "eager for base gain," turning the opportunities of their office into a means of personal profit.

Paul is not content with outward blamelessness in the conduct of the deacons; they must also possess a vital spiritual life. They must be known as "holding the mystery of the faith." The expression, "the mystery of the faith," occurs only here. A "mystery" in Scripture is not something mysterious and incomprehensible but a truth before unknown but now divinely revealed to the believer (cf. I Cor. 2:7-10). The definitive genetive "of the faith" may be differently interpreted. It may be regarded as denoting the substance of the mystery, that is the content of the Christian Gospel, "*the* faith." Or it may have a subjective sense as pointing to the revealed truth which is apprehended and appropriated by faith. Either view is possible and amounts to about the same thing. This mystery is a precious treasure which is best preserved in the casket of "a pure conscience." He who would commend the truths of the Gospel to others must conscientiously exemplify it in his own conduct.

2) The testing of deacons, v. 10. "And let these also first be proved." The "also" indicates that the deacons, no less than the elders, must be tested before being placed into office. (The testing of the elders, although not stated before, is self-evident from the requirements laid down concerning them.) They are to be "proved," tested like metals to show their genuineness, and having met the test, are to be approved for the office. The use of the present tense, rather than the aorist which would have implied a formal test, indicates the testing as covering a con-

siderable period of time. It does not mean that the candidates for the deaconship are to be placed on probation, tried out in office before being given permanent appointment. The reference is rather to the general judgment formed by the Christian community of the character and conduct of those men who may be available for appointment to the office. Having been known as "blameless" or unaccused in their Christian life, they can be appointed to serve.

3) The qualifications of the women (*deaconesses*), v. 11. "Women in like manner." The Greek is as indefinite as this English translation. The reference cannot be to women generally since Paul is here dealing with church officers. Two views are held: (1) the wives of the deacons, or (2) the deaconesses of the church. The former interpretation is introduced into the King James rendering, "Even so must *their* wives." (The Greek has no word for "their" with the word *gunaikas*, "wives," or "women.") On this view the insistence upon the qualifications of the deacon's wife may be regarded as necessary since his wife would naturally lend a helping hand in the care of the poor and the sick. But the preponderance of evidence is for the latter view. The words "in like manner," also used to introduce the discussion about deacons, suggest the introduction of a separate class; each group alike must meet certain qualifications. The qualifications here required correspond, with appropriate variations, to the personal qualifications required of deacons. The statement places the personal qualifications of these "women" on a level with those required of the men deacons. If the reference is to the wives of the deacons it would have been more appropriately introduced in connection with the domestic qualifications of the deacons. The ancient interpreters generally took the view that the reference is to deaconesses. The New Testament gives indication that deaconesses existed in some apostolic churches. Phoebe is called "a deacon of the church that is at Cenchrea" (Rom. 16:1, Gr.). "We cannot doubt that the neces-

sity for special service of women among women was early felt in the church, and that a regular order of deaconesses had been appointed before the date of this epistle" (Pope).

The first qualification mentioned is the general character requirement "grave" or "dignified" (cf. v. 8 for the deacons). The one negative qualification is "not slanderers," literally "not devils," throwing across accusations at others. Two positive qualifications follow, "temperate," or "sober" (see 3:2) and "faithful in all things." The latter is a general statement emphasizing the need for trustworthiness in all matters entrusted to them, whether great or small.

4) The domestic qualifications of deacons, v. 12. These correspond to the high standard laid down for the bishop (see vv. 4, 5 above).

c. The reward of faithful service, v. 13. By rendering "have served well *as deacons*" our versions limit the reference of the verse. It seems better not to limit the verb here to its technical meaning but to interpret it generally of any service done to others. Thus viewed it forms a fitting conclusion to the entire discussion about church officers. As an incentive to faithful service, it holds up the reward for such service, whether by bishop or deacons. The reward comes to those who "have served well" or "ministered excellently." The reference is not necessarily to the whole earthly life but to some definite period during which such service was rendered (aorist tense). They thereby "gain" or "are acquiring" for themselves "a good standing." The word "standing" means "a step" and so denotes an advanced position. Paul is not speaking of the ecclesiastical advancement of the deacon to the overseership, nor is he speaking of the future reward in glory. The reference is to the excellent community standing and recognition which they require through their having rendered good service. They further acquire "great boldness in the faith which is in Christ Jesus." The consciousness of personal integrity and community acceptance enables them to speak and act with boldness and assurance.

3. The Personal Word to Timothy in View of Christian Truth, 3:14-16

In concluding this second main division Paul again turns to Timothy with a personal word to him. "These things" has reference to the instructions contained in chapters 2 and 3. In glancing back over these instructions Paul pauses to indicate his purpose in writing them to Timothy (vv. 14, 15a), briefly touches on the nature of the church where they are to be observed (v. 15b), and concludes with a majestic summary of the substance of Christian truth (v. 16).

a. The purpose in writing to Timothy, vv. 14-15a.

Paul had left Timothy at his station at Ephesus (1:2). As he writes he hopes to be able to return to Ephesus shortly. (Many manuscripts read "more quickly," that is, more quickly than the writing of the letter might lead Timothy to suppose.) But it was probable that circumstances might delay his return. This possibility of delay induced him to write out these instructions in order that "thou mayest know how men ought to behave themselves in the house of God." The absence of any pronoun in the original makes it possible to insert either "thou," as in the King James Version, or "men," as in the American Standard Version. Since the preceding instructions dealt not merely with Timothy's duty but with the character and conduct of the church officials, the general term may be preferable. But it makes little difference which is inserted since Timothy's "behavior" or "manner of life" in carrying out the instructions would affect the behavior of the church. "The house of God" does not mean a church building, a meaning which it never has in the New Testament, but rather the members of the church themselves who compose God's house, since He indwells the Church. The reference may be either to the Church Universal or to the local church.

b. The nature of the church, v. 15b. Paul continues with a

statement about the nature of the Church as explaining why there should be a befitting behavior on the part of the members of the church. Reverent and becoming conduct is due because it is "the church of the living God." This reference to "the living God" gives a pointed contrast to the dead idols enshrined in pagan temples and ministered to by their devotees. But the living God is the author and source of all life; He constantly cares for and guides all in connection with His church.

Paul further describes the church as "the pillar and ground of the truth." Here the figure changes in that the temple is no longer the church but "the truth," the great doctrinal content of the Christian revelation. "Pillar and ground" indicate the function of the church in relation to the Gospel. It is a "pillar" of the truth in that it holds up and supports it before the world. The church is also the stay and buttress (this is a better rendering than "ground") of God's truth in that it supports and maintains it in opposition to all attacks upon it.

c. The substance of Christian truth, v. 16. The content of the truth which the church upholds, supports, and confesses is summarized in the last verse. "Without controversy" is literally "confessedly great"—it is a matter to be openly confessed, that is the mission of the church. "The mystery of godliness" means the revelation of the truth which godliness embraces and on which it rests. The remainder of the verse, generally regarded as a quotation from a Christian hymn, depicts its contents. This "mystery" is really Christ Jesus Himself. "He who was manifested." Space forbids a discussion of the critical problem of the verse. The weight of the textual evidence lies with the reading "who" (*hos*), rather than "God" on the one hand, or "which" (referring to "mystery") on the other. The unexpressed antecedent is Christ Himself, as the quotation shows. It is composed of six brief lines, taking us all the way from the Incarnation to the ascension of Christ. Some would group them into three pairs, but it seems better to divide the whole into two parts, each with three clauses. Lock outlines the contents as follows:

(1) The Life of the Incarnate—	
(a) as seen on earth,	"Manifested in the flesh,
	Justified in the spirit,
(b) as watched from heaven,	Seen of angels,
(2) The Life of the Ascended Lord—	
(a) as preached on earth,	Preached among the nations,
	Believed on in the world,
(b) as lived in heaven,	Received up in glory."

The words "manifested in the flesh" are a statement of the Incarnation and imply an unveiling of a previous existence. "Justified in the spirit" refers to the vindication of His claims when God raised Him from the dead. Men rejected and crucified Him as a criminal but in the resurrection God reversed the verdict of men. "Seen of angels" apparently means that they watched His earthly life as God incarnate (Luke 2:13; Mark 1:13; John 1:51; Luke 24:23, etc.). "Preached among the nations, believed on in the world" sets before us the great evangelistic mission of the church in which Paul himself was so zealously active. "Received up in glory" refers not only to the fact of the ascension but also denotes the fact of His ascension "in glory," the glorious character of the One who ascended.

This majestic summary of Christian truth forms a fitting climax to the second division of the Epistle dealing with church order. It forms also an appropriate setting for the grim subject of the coming apostasy in the next chapter.

III. THE ADVICE TO TIMOTHY IN VIEW OF THE CHARGE, 4:1-6:2

WITH CHAPTER FOUR we begin the third main division of the Epistle. Here Paul offers Timothy some constructive advice in carrying out the charge committed to him. The advice relates to his personal work in view of the coming apostasy (4:1-16), as well as to his official work with various groups within the churches (5:1-6:2).

1. His Personal Work in View of the Apostasy, 4:1-16

The opening "but" introduces a contrast between the sublime mystery of redemption which the church confesses as the norm of Christian faith (3:16) and the coming departure from the faith of which the Spirit warns. Timothy must carry on his work in the clear consciousness of this grim prospect. Paul sets forth the objective warning concerning the coming apostasy (vv. 1-5), and then indicates to Timothy that he is to find subjective fortification through a faithful ministry (vv. 6-11) and a becoming conduct as a minister (vv. 12-16).

a. The objective warning against false teaching, vv. 1-5. Timothy must work under the realization of the fact that along with the believing reception being accorded to the preaching of the Gospel in many quarters there will come a definite falling away from the faith which its proclamation awakened. This is a revelation of vital significance today, and neither minister nor people can afford to remain uninformed about the apostasy. In speaking of this coming apostasy Paul mentions the Spirit's precise prediction of it (v. 1a), gives a characterization of the apostates (vv. 1b, 2), and indicates the erroneous nature of their teaching (vv. 3-5).

1) The prediction of the apostasy, v. 1a. "The Spirit saith expressly." The Holy Spirit Himself, the Spirit of prophecy, is the author of the prediction, and it is uttered "expressly." that is, clearly and explicitly. Such an apostasy was clearly indicated in the prophetic utterances of Christ, but the reference here is to a specific revelation being made by the Spirit. Whether it came to Paul himself or to some other New Testament prophets is not indicated. In II Thessalonians 2 Paul himself gives us a fuller unfolding of this apostasy. The present tense "saith" indicates that it was being given more than once. The emphasis is placed not on the prophet but on the inspired prediction. The time of the prophecy is given as "in later times," in times future to the speaker. No particular time is thus set, but evidently the beginnings of the apostasy were in the near future. The full and tragic culmination of the apostasy will be reached in the closing days of this dispensation. The essence of the prediction is that "some shall fall away from the faith." "The faith" here denotes the doctrinal truths of the Christian faith. The verb "fall away," or "apostatize," denotes not an unintentional fall but a deliberate withdrawal from the faith once professed. An apostate is not one who gives up his profession of being a Christian, but one who forsakes the truth of the Christian faith.

2) The characterization of the apostates, vv. 1b, 2. The apostates are described as "giving heed to seducing spirits and doctrines of demons." The words "giving heed to" mean not merely to give attention to but to give assent to. As soon as men turn away from Christ and His truth they pass under the influence of "seducing spirits." It has well been said that man never

stands isolated; if he is not subject to the influence of the Holy Spirit, he at once falls under the power of seducing spirits. These "seducing spirits," spirits that lead astray and deceive, are not the false teachers but the evil spirits animating them. Paul here clearly indicates the superhuman element in doctrinal error. "Doctrines of demons" does not mean doctrines about demons, but doctrines which the demons teach. They influence the minds of men to give heed to erroneous teaching. The word is not "devils," for Scripture speaks of only one Devil, but rather "demons," a word never applied to Satan in Scripture. "Demons" are evil beings, the agents of Satan, marshaled and commanded by "the prince of the power of the air" in his ceaseless war against the kingdom of God. In I Corinthians 10:20 Paul connects them with the idolatry and delusions of heathenism. These teaching demons are the ultimate source of doctrinal heresy.

Paul next indicates the human element in the apostasy by describing the men who are the tools of the seducing spirits. The evil spirits work and their teachings are exhibited "through the hypocrisy of men that speak lies." Their hypocrisy lays them open to demonic influences and provides the atmosphere in which they can work. These men pretended to spiritually inspired lives but were dominated by a false spiritualism. They wore a mask of holiness which they considered was derived from their false asceticism and abstinence from things legitimate. Behind their deception lay the corruption of their hearts. They were in a state (perfect tense) of being "branded in their own conscience as with a hot iron." The figure in this translation is derived from the penal practice of branding certain criminals on their forehead. So these hypocrites, with their outward show of holiness and extreme asceticism, have the brand of guilt resting on their conscience. The rendering in the King James Version, "seared as with a hot iron," points rather to the effect that their sin has produced on their conscience. Through their hypocrisy their conscience, from constant violation, has become seared and rendered incapable of further feeling the compunctions of conscience. This view seems preferable.

3) The teaching of the apostates, vv. 3-5. Paul points out two specimens of their erroneous teaching (v. 3a) and adds his refutation (vv. 3b-5).

a) The nature of the teaching, v. 3a. From a consideration of the character of the false teachers Paul passes to a refutation of their teaching. Two examples of their false asceticism are given. "Forbidding to marry, *and commanding* to abstain from meats." The words in italics are rightly added to bring out the meaning.

The two points mentioned characterize the teaching as marked by a false asceticism. Abstinence from marriage is regarded as a means to a higher sanctity, thus placing the celibate life on a higher spiritual level than the married life. The practice of abstaining from certain foods, and perhaps all foods at certain seasons, is esteemed meritorious and a special virtue.

The picture presented is a prophecy. The point is not how soon these teachings would arise but that they would arise. The germs of this teaching were already active during apostolic times among the Essenes. Gradually they mingled with similar principles derived from other systems until at last, after the apostolic age, they became embodied in a fuller and wider Gnosticism. It found expression in the whole monastic system and is still flourishing in Roman Catholicism and other systems of false asceticism.

b) The refutation of the teaching, vv. 3b-5. Having mentioned these teachings, the apostle at once launches into a refutation. Usually the neuter "which things" is referred only to "meats." Then reasons are sought why Paul did not deal with the problem of marriage. It seems best to regard the neuter plural relative pronoun as including both marriage and foods. The teaching on both points was contrary to the creative purpose of God. "Which God created to be received with thanksgiving." The words "to be received" translate a noun meaning "participation, taking," thus indicating that God meant for us to participate, to share in these things which He has created. But these teachers would prohibit us from participating in them. The participation is to be "with thanksgiving" in due recognition of them as God's good gifts. He created them for the benefit of "them that believe and know the truth," that is, the believers. The half-instructed, "weak" brother has not yet come into the full realization of the divine purpose concerning these things.

This false teaching is inconsistent with the divine beneficence in creation. "For every creature of God is good." It would be better to render "creation," since "creature" for us today denotes that which lives and moves. God Himself instituted the marriage relation and created food to sustain life. The creation of God is "good," hence "nothing is to be rejected," or "thrown away." When men reject that which is God's creation and intended for their good, they only reveal their ignorance and willfullness.

With the opening "for" of verse 5 Paul explains what Christian thanksgiving does as these things are thankfully received. "They are sanctified through the word of God and prayer." Thanksgiving is not a magical formula which changes the nature of these things but it gives a sacred value to them as gifts whose source might otherwise be overlooked. The additional clause, "through the word of God and prayer," defines the twofold sanctifying medium. By "the word of God" Paul may mean that the Scriptures justify our use of these things by direct sanction. Others think the reference is to the use of scriptural language in the expression of our thanks. "Prayer," translated "intercessions" in 2:1, denotes prayer as free and open speech with God. The reference is not to any specific prayer formula but rather to that constant habit of referring everything to God as the Giver of every good and perfect gift. The two are distinct and yet closely united. "When the revelation which God has given us in Scripture is met by the lowly and prayerful attitude in our hearts—then a sanctification falls upon appetite and passion; they are kept in their proper place, and purged by the Divine Spirit. Incontinence becomes as hateful on the one hand as asceticism is ungrateful on the other" (Horton).

Paul's words certainly sanction the Christian practice of grace before meals. To eat without giving thanks is base ingratitude. But the scope of the passage is much wider than that.

b. The subjective fortification against error, vv. 6-16. Having set forth the fact of the coming apostasy, Paul tells Timothy how to fortify himself and the churches under his care against error. He is to find fortification through a faithful ministry (vv. 6-11) and through becoming personal conduct (vv. 12-16).

1) The fortification through a faithful ministry, vv. 6-11. Paul holds up before Timothy the ideal of being "a good minister of Christ Jesus." Our word "minister" today generally refers to an ordained clergyman. But that is not the meaning of the word here. It is the word rendered "deacon" in 3:8. It means one who serves, the emphasis being not upon his status but on his activity. Paul draws the picture of "an excellent servant of Christ Jesus" by describing his characteristics (v. 6), activities (vv. 7-9), motivation (v. 10), and duty (v. 11).

a) The characteristics of a good minister, v. 6. He is characterized by his concern for the welfare of others. "If thou put the brethren in mind of these things." The Greek is a participial construction and does not imply any doubt. It points out in what way he will be a good minister in relation to others, "by submitting these things to the brethren." "These things" has reference to 4:1-5. He is to fortify the brethren against the apostasy by putting and keeping them on their guard against the danger. In relationship to himself he must be characterized as being "nourished in the words of the faith and the good doctrine." The statements that embody what is believed, the excellent doctrinal formulations of the Christian faith in which he has been instructed, are to be the "daily bread" upon which his soul is nourished. Perhaps the voice of the verb is middle, "nourishing thyself." Every good minister must take care to nourish his own soul on the truths which he is supplying to others. It is quite possible for him to become so busy finding food for the flock that he fails to nourish his own soul with the food he prepares. Paul gives Timothy high praise by adding, "which thou hast followed *until now*." The perfect tense states that throughout Timothy has faithfully adhered to the true doctrine of the faith. Fidelity to the truth we have already gained is the best preparation for the realization of higher attainments.

b) The activity of a good minister, vv. 7-9. It is best with the King James Version to put a period at the end of verse 6 and relate the first part of verse 7 with what follows. The negative action commanded in verse 7a is thus set in appropriate contrast to the positive action in what follows (vv. 7b-9).

(1) Neg.—The refusal of myths, v. 7a. "But refuse profane and old wives' fables." The reference is not to 4:1-5, for that is still future, but to 1:4. Timothy already has people coming to him with these fables. In disdain Paul characterizes them as "profane and old wives' fables." The first adjective points out that there is nothing sacred about them, while the other indicates their futile, senseless nature; they are nothing but silly fictions, fit only for senile, childish old crones to chatter about. When people bring them to him he is to "refuse," "beg off" dealing with them. To discuss them seriously would be to give them a dignity which they do not deserve. The present tense indicates this as his constant reaction.

(2) Pos.—The exercising of himself unto godliness, vv. 7b-9. "And," or better "but," instead of occupying himself with such fruitless activity, Timothy is urged to "exercise thyself unto godliness." His chief concern both for himself and for the members of the churches is to be that active, healthy practical piety

which ever seeks personal holiness and is completely devoted to God. The present tense means that he is to "keep on exercising" himself thus, as he is now doing. As the Greek athlete disciplines his body with strenuous exercise and rigorous training, so Timothy is to discipline himself in godliness.

The "for" in verse 8 introduces an explanation for this exhortation. "For bodily exercise is profitable for a little; but godliness is profitable for all things." Two views are taken as to the meaning of "bodily exercise." Many take it to mean physical exercise, gymnastics, athletic training. On this view Paul uses it as an illustration from the physical realm to contrast the superiority of discipline in godliness. Others regard it as a reference to asceticism, the mortification of the body for religious purposes, as in the abstinence from marriage and meats. This view is more in harmony with the context where asceticism has been dealt with and its undue exaltation is deprecated. While Paul eschewed unreal and extreme forms of bodily discipline, he did not disapprove of it in every form. He acknowledged that it profited "for a little." Paul himself disciplined his body to keep it in subjection (I Cor. 9:27) and was "in fastings often" (II Cor. 11:27). Keeping the body with all of its desires and passions under discipline is worth something, is in fact a part of a true life of godliness. But it is only a small part, for true godliness has its seat in the spirit, not in bodily discipline. Godliness is not achieved through a rigorous mortification of the body in order to control the spirit, it is rather the spiritual in control of the body. "Godliness is profitable for all things," for the entire well-being, physical and spiritual, temporal and eternal. Its supreme advantage is that it has attached to it "the promise of life." The word for "life" is *zoē*, the higher principle of life, rather than *bios*, the means of life, that which sustains and supports life here. Here is no guarantee for the worldly prosperity of the godly. But it does make for "a true well-being in this life and obtains life's real good, since it places man in right relations to God and the world, and fits him for the true enjoyment of all earthly good" (Harvey). It also insures the highest well-being in the life to come. "The pursuit of piety is not hampered by the interposition of death. This great change only bestows upon it its ultimate and perfect reward" (Lilley).

The words of verse 9, "Faithful is the saying," are best regarded as referring to what precedes rather than to what follows. They constitute the apostolic seal upon what has just been said about the superiority of godliness. "Those who have faith have found this saying trustworthy, and it is worth all men's while to accept it" (Lock). (See 1:15.)

c) The motivation of the good minister, v. 10. "For to this end we labor," that is, in order that the promise which godliness has may be fulfilled in us. This goal provides the motivation or inspiration of the good minister. With this goal before us, "we labor and strive." The "we" unites Timothy with Paul in this motivation. The reading in the King James Version "and suffer reproach" is based on a different reading which seems less suited to the context. The word "labor" speaks of toil to the point of exhaustion, while the verb "strive," from which we get our word "agonize," carries the picture of the athlete putting in the last ounce of his energy into the race in order victoriously to reach the goal. Paul "and his companions had such a deep sense of the grandeur of the reward held out in the Gospel, that they counted no labor too heavy, no agony too severe, that led them gradually but surely to the expected goal. The life of a faithful minister of Christ can never be entirely easy" (Lilley).

The reason why they thus labor and strive is "because we have our hope set on the living God." The construction (*epi* with the locative) pictures the hope as resting on God as the only true foundation of hope. The perfect tense indicates that this hope has permanently been set on "the living God." "Their hope is not fixed on the dead idols of heathenism, but on the true and living God, who is himself life and the Fountain of life, and who is, therefore, able to fulfill his word" (Harvey). As the source of all life He is also the Giver of all saving grace. The demonstration of the saving activity of God in human lives makes this hope all the more sure. Paul accordingly thinks of Him as "the Saviour of all men, specially of them that believe." The concluding phrase shows that God is not the Saviour of unbelievers in the same sense that He is of believers. This statement cannot be used to support an unscriptural universalism which teaches that all men will be saved. "God is Saviour of all men, by His intention, offer, and propitiatory work (I John 2:2). But as on man's side that salvation can only be realized by faith, His saving relation to those who believe is something over and above His relation to all. He saves all potentially—those who believe, actually" (Horton).

d) The duty of the good minister, v. 11. "These things command and teach." "These things" refers to all that Paul has said in verses 6-10. He has written them for the express purpose that Timothy may "command and teach" them to the congregations under his supervision. The tense (present) denotes that this is to be his regular practice. "Command" suggests the authoritative transmission of these matters, while "teach" indicates that they are doctrinal matters which must be inculcated in the mind and thinking of the hearers.

2) The fortification through becoming conduct as a minister, vv. 12-16. To be effective the service of a minister of Christ Jesus must be undergirded by a conduct becoming to a minister. His conduct will be a further source of security to Timothy. Paul indicates the nature of his duties (vv. 12-14) and then earnestly urges the fulfillment of those duties (vv. 15, 16).

a) The indication of his personal duties, vv. 12-14. In rapid succession Paul lays before Timothy three duties which are incumbent upon him as a good minister of Christ Jesus. It is his responsibility to make his youth respected because of his example (v. 12), to attend to the public services (v. 13), and to exercise his gift (v. 14).

(1) To make his youth respected because of his example, v. 12. "Let no man despise thy youth." We can only guess at the age of Timothy at this time, but he must have been between thirty and forty years old. Many of the elders with whom Timothy was dealing would be much older than he. As compared to Paul, whose representative he was at the time, Timothy was indeed a young man for his responsible task. But Paul did not think him too young and says so. He must not allow others to "despise" him because of his youth. The verb "connotes that the contempt felt in the mind is displayed in injurious action" (White). He is not to allow them to push him around because of his youth.

"But be thou an ensample to them that believe." This positive injunction balances the previous negative. His life is to be such as will hush every adverse reaction about his youth. The rendering of the King James, "an example of believers," is better. "Timothy was to be not merely an ensample *to* believers, but an exemplar *of* them (Gr. gen.) by manifesting in his own life all the graces of an ideal believer" (Lilley). It is the first duty of a minister to display in his own life that which he wishes his people to be.

Paul names five things (not six, for the addition "in spirit" in the King James Version lacks manuscript authority) in which Timothy is to be the example. The repetition of the preposition makes each distinct. The first two, "in word, in manner of life," relate to outward conduct. "Word" has reference to his speech, whether in public or in private discourse, while "manner of life" points to his personal conduct. The familiar "conversation" in the King James is now misleading since by common usage it has come to be limited to intercourse in speech. The remaining three relate to the inner life. "In love" relates to love to God as well as men; it is the motivating power of the Christian life.

"In faith, in purity" picture the inward disposition. From the context it seems probable that "faith" here has the passive sense of "fidelity, trustworthiness." "Purity" speaks not of personal chastity but of purity of intention, sincerity of character. Others take "faith" in its usual meaning, with love as the second pair, and interpret "purity" as the concluding element denoting the nature of the life rooted in love and faith.

(2) To attend to the public services, v. 13. The words "Till I come" clearly place Timothy at Ephesus as the apostolic representative in Paul's absence. In regard to the public services in the assemblies under his supervision, he is to "give heed," give attention "to reading, to exhortation, to teaching." The definite article with each noun should be reproduced in translation. "The reading" refers not to Timothy's personal reading and study, important as that is, but to the public reading of the Scriptures in the assembly (cf. Luke 4:16-17; Acts 13:15). This would include the Old Testament and doubtless such books of the New Testament as were already available (cf. Col. 4:16; I Thess. 5:27; II Peter 3:15, 16). It is Timothy's duty to see not that something is read but what is read. The reason for this Lenski states as follows:

> The present danger was, that here and there some of the cranks and fanatics (1:4) and the foolish law-teachers (1:7) might read, or ask to have read, as lections the Old Testament genealogies, to which to pin their myths, and lections from the Levitical laws, to be interpreted for their ignorant purposes. This Timothy was not to allow.

"The exhortation" refers to the public address which followed the reading of the Scriptures and was intended to appeal to the conscience and will of the hearers and lead to appropriate action. "The teaching," or better, "the doctrine," refers to the instructional content of the message given, informing and enlightening the intellect of the hearers. In both of these matters

Timothy is to exercise oversight to insure that they are not mis-used by the would-be teachers to inculcate error in the congregations.

(3) To exercise his gift, v. 14. A third duty Paul urges on Timothy, "Neglect not the gift that is in thee." "Neglect not," or better "be not careless about" is a negative substitute for a positive injunction, "be diligently attending to." The exhortation does not imply blame on Timothy's part. But this gift is not a charm which is supposed to act by itself; it requires the co-operation of its possessor. God's gifts to us, whether of nature or of grace, can be neglected, and their neglect is a sin.

"The gift" is not Timothy's office itself, as "in thee" shows. It is rather Timothy's God-given ability to understand the Gospel and to discern error, as well as his authority to control others. The bestowal of this gift on Timothy Paul indicates thus, "which was given thee by prophecy, with the laying on of the hands of the presbytery." God gave him the gift "by prophecy," some specific utterance of the Spirit which designated him as its recipient. The gift was imparted in connection with (*meta*) "the laying on of the hands of the presbytery." "The presbytery" is a collective term denoting the body of elders or presbyters in a local congregation, each congregation apparently having several (cf. Acts 14:23; Titus 1:5). Views are divided as to the time and place referred to. The common view takes it as a reference to the ordination of Timothy at Lystra (Acts 16:1-3). Others think the laying on of hands here mentioned took place in Ephesus when Timothy was induced into the office of bishop. But this misconceives Timothy's position at Ephesus. If we locate it in Ephesus, much more probable is the view that it relates to the time when Paul placed Timothy at Ephesus as his representative (1:3). On this view Paul's placement of Timothy over the Asian congregations as his representative was not an autocratic act taken by Paul alone, but was done with the sanction of the leaders of these churches.

b) The exhortations diligently to fulfill these duties, vv. 15, 16. Paul earnestly presses upon Timothy the fulfillment of these duties by means of four present imperatives. The present tense means that he is to continue doing these things as he now is. These imperatives are grouped into two pairs, each pair followed by an explanatory clause.

Paul appeals for a wholehearted occupation with "these things," those set forth in verses 12-14. "Be diligent in these things; give thyself wholly to them." The first verb may mean either "to study, ponder, meditate on" or "to attend to, care for, practice." Either is suitable here, but the context favors the latter meaning. Paul is calling for careful thought in the practice of these things. "Give thyself wholly to them" is literally, "go on being in them." They are entirely to absorb and engross him. We might say, "Be wrapped up in them." The stated reason for the appeal is, "that thy progress may be manifest to all." It marks the purpose or contemplated result of his wholehearted occupation with these duties. The word "progress" ("profit" in the King James is inadequate) contains the graphic picture of a pioneer cutting his way forward through obstacles by means of strenuous effort, like a man blazing a trail through a tangled forest. The usual interpretation is that Timothy is to show such progress in his Christian life and ministerial activities that the people will clearly notice that progress and thus be led to think well of the young man. Then the recognition of the progress is thought of as still future. But Timothy is no longer a young man just beginning his ministerial career. The thought seems rather to be that by his diligent fulfillment of these duties the people will recognize the progress that Timothy has made since the day when they first learned to know him at Ephesus as Paul's young helper. The recognition on their part of this development in him would convince them that Paul had not made a mistake in selecting him for his responsible position.

A second pair of imperatives follows, calling for thoughtful perseverance in these duties. "Take heed to thyself and to thy teaching." The reference to himself connects with verse 12, while "the teaching" (Gr.) relates to verse 13. There is an intimate connection between a minister's personality and his message. His first care is his own personal life, he must give thought to his position of responsibility properly to fulfill it. "The teaching" includes not only his own presentation of truth but also his responsibility for the teaching of others in the congregations. "Continue in them," or "abide in them." These duties are to be the sphere of his life and activity.

The result of this thoughtful perseverance will be, "in doing this thou shalt save both thyself and them that hear thee." This is the great incentive set before him. Notice that the salvation is not procured "by doing" but "in doing" this. We are not saved by our faithful performance of our duties, but the faithful performance of our duties is the sphere within which our salvation is realized. A pastor unfaithful in doctrine and morals is saving neither himself nor his congregation. Salvation here means more than preservation from false teaching, although that is included. Salvation here has its full soteriological significance.

2. His Official Work with Various Groups, 5:1-6:2

From the advice given Timothy personally, in relation to his work as a good minister of Christ Jesus, Paul turns to advise him in relation to his official work with various groups in the congregations. He advises Timothy briefly concerning his attitude in dealing with varied individual members (5:1-2), instructs him at considerable length in regard to widows (5:3-16), discusses his duty in relation to the elders (5:17-25), and concludes with a word about the instructions to be given to the slaves (6:1, 2).

a. The attitude in dealing with individual members, 5:1, 2. Before giving counsel relative to his official work with different groups, Paul reminds Timothy of the attitude appropriate in dealing with different individuals in the congregation, viewed according to age and sex. "Rebuke not an elder." The correlative terms employed make it clear that by "elder" Paul here means not an official of the church but an old man. The statement implies that there is something remiss in the man's life. Even old age does not shield from folly. In such cases Timothy, remembering his own youth, is not to withhold correction but is to administer it without unbecoming sharpness or harshness. The verb "rebuke" literally means "to strike, beat with blow," then metaphorically the force is "to pound with words, to reprimand." The aorist tense signifies that he is not to start doing such a thing. "But exhort him as a father." He must have respect for age and admonish him as a right-minded young man would a father who has erred.

This second verb is in thought supplied with each of the following groups. The present tense indicates that this is to be his habitual attitude in dealing with all cases that may occur. "The younger men as brothers" reminds him that he is to avoid all show of self-exaltation over them because of his position. Paul's mention of father, brothers, mothers, sisters, shows that he is thinking of the church as a family and each member must be treated with family affection. Grammatically the words "in all purity" may be related to the verb "exhort," thus indicating that all his admonitions must be administered in a manner which is above censure or suspicion. In the highest degree is this necessary in his dealings with the young women. What miserable scandals would have been avoided in all ages if young ministers had always heeded Paul's admonition!

b. The duty in regard to widows, 5:3-16. With verse 3 Paul passes to a consideration of widows as a particular group with whom Timothy will officially have to deal. The matter has several ramifications and is dealt with at considerable length. The passage is not without its difficulties of interpretation. Paul discusses the duty of supporting widows (vv. 3-8), instructs Timothy in regard those who are to be enrolled (vv. 9-15), and concludes with a statement about the duty of a believing woman toward widowed relatives (v. 16).

1) The duty of supporting widows, vv. 3-8. Structurally, verses 3-8 form a unit; a connective particle joins sentence to sentence. Paul begins with a command to honor genuine widows (v. 3), explains by means of a definitive classification of widows (vv. 4-6), and concludes with instructions concerning parental support (vv. 7, 8).

a) The command to honor genuine widows, v. 3. "Honor widows that are widows indeed." The basic thought in the word "widow" is that of loneliness. The word comes from an adjective meaning "bereft" and speaks of her resultant loneliness as having been bereft of her husband. The added word "indeed" places the emphasis upon those whose circumstances are characteristic of real widowhood. We might have expected Paul to say, "Sympathize with genuine widows," but instead he says "Honor." It is somewhat difficult to determine the exact force of the word here. In the light of the preceding verses it seems natural to give it its regular significance of showing respect and esteem. On the other hand, what follows shows that the problem of the support of widows is in the apostle's mind, hence it is generally held that with the word Paul implies a loving provision for their needs. It seems that the thought of *respect* was primarily in the writer's mind, but the word "honor" easily lent itself to the expression of the thought of *support*, a matter which immediately follows. If so, the word used "suggests that such relief is not to be dealt out to them as to mere paupers, in a manner to degrade them, but as to Christian women whom the Church holds in honor, and to whom it thus shows honor" (Harvey).

b) The definitive classification of widows, vv. 4-6. Paul defines what he means by a "widow indeed." There are two other kinds of widows who do not fall within his definition. One kind is mentioned before and the other after his description of a genuine widow.

(1) The widow having children, v. 4. "But if any widow hath children or grandchildren." Thus she is not characterized as being truly desolate. Her descendants have a duty toward their mother or grandmother. When the King James Version was translated the word "nephews" meant grandchildren, but that meaning has now become obsolete. The Greek word means "sprung from one," that is, offspring or descendants. "Let them [that is, the descendants, not the widow as some would interpret] learn first to show piety toward their own family, and to requite their parents." It is their duty toward their widowed mother or grandmother "to show piety." This infinitive means "to act reverently and dutifully," while the following infinitive, "to requite their parents," indicates more specifically what is involved. The word "parents" means "forebearers, one's living ancestors," and thus included mother and grandmother. "To requite" may more literally be rendered "to be duly rendering back recompense." The children owe their parents a great debt which they can never fully repay for all the love, patience, and self-sacrificing care bestowed upon them during their infancy and childhood. For them to make this requittal "is acceptable in the sight of God."

(2) The widow who is a genuine widow, v. 5. In contrast to the widow with children Paul places the genuine widow whom he characterizes as "desolate," that is, in a permanent state of being left alone and forsaken. She is without children or relatives to whom she may look for support. In her desolation she "hath her hope set on God," the God who in His Word has made many promises to just such sadly bereft widows. The construction (*epi* with the accusative) indicates that her hope is directed toward God, while the perfect tense points to the abiding character of her Godward hope. With her thoughts turned Godward, she ever "continueth in supplications and

prayers." (On these words see 2:1.) In her supplications she continually makes known her needs to God, while in her prayers of worship and communion she approaches God when worry and care would assail her. And this she does "night and day." She allows no portion of her life to be unmarked by her prayers. Unlike verse 4, this verse is a descriptive statement and not a command. She does not have to be told to do these things, she does them without being told.

(3) The widow living in pleasure, v. 6. By contrast the apostle pictures another kind of widow, the worst class of all. "She that giveth herself to pleasure." The words translate an articular present feminine participle, "the one living luxuriously or self-indulgently." She is what would today be called a "fast" and "gay" widow. Paul's verdict is that she is "dead while she liveth." "Her frivolous, selfish, sensual existence is not true life; it fills none of life's true ends; and, as to any real value to herself or to others, she is practically dead" (Lipscomb and Shepherd). She is alive in the flesh but is dead spiritually.

c) The instructions concerning parental support, vv. 7, 8. "These things also command." The Greek word for "also" stands at the beginning of the sentence and makes this verse a definite part of the preceding verses. Hence by "these things" are meant all the matters mentioned in the paragraph so far. These things were not written merely for Timothy's personal guidance; he is to pass them on to the entire congregation so that all the members concerned, being properly informed, "may be without reproach."

If all the members are to be "without reproach," this matter of parental support cannot be neglected. It is one aspect of this whole matter concerning widows which Timothy must command. "If any provideth not for his own, and specially his own household." The form of the conditional sentence (first class) implies that Paul was aware that some were prone to this failure. Apparently they were trying to escape the personal responsibility of parental support by seeking to shift the responsibility onto the church. "His own" are his relatives, while "his own household" are all those who in any way form part of his household. The verb "provideth" means "to think of beforehand," and then to prepare for the need foreseen. It is a Christian duty thus to foresee and to provide for one's dependents. The primary reference here is to the obligation of children and grandchildren to support their widowed ancestors. But the statement is sufficiently general also to include the duty of parents to provide for their children. "So far from relaxing the mutual obligations of family life, the acceptance of the message of Christianity only tended to make them stronger and closer" (Lilley). Failure to fulfill this obligation Paul judges sharply. "He hath denied the faith." Such a gross violation of the teaching of Christianity is a practical denial of that faith. There can be no separation between vital faith and personal conduct. A living faith affords a rule of Christian conduct. Paul stamps the person who fails to fulfill this obligation as "worse than an unbeliever," because the unbeliever, fulfilling the law of nature, does what he, with the higher revelation of grace, fails to do. (The rendering "infidel" of the King James Version is stronger than the original which does not have the sting attached to "infidel" as implying a deliberate rejection of religion.)

2) The instructions concerning the enrollment of widows, vv. 9-15. "Let none be enrolled as a widow—" These words at once raise a problem of interpretation. What is meant by this enrollment? The verb itself means "to set down in a list, to register, enroll" like soldiers, citizens, etc., who are thus classed together and distinguished from those not thus listed. One class of expositors, taking their cue from the early Church Fathers, hold that the reference is to "ecclesiastical widows," widows who were appointed by the church to perform certain acts of charity, such as the care of orphans, the supervision of the younger members of their own sex, etc., and as such constituted

an official, or at least a semiofficial group in the church. Others, refusing to read Paul's words in the light of subsequent historical developments, see a reference only to an enrollment of widows who could legitimately be regarded as being entitled to the support of the church. We accept the latter view as the more probable.

The fact that a "roll" or "list" is mentioned does not prove that any ecclesiastical order is being referred to. At most it shows that the matter of the support of widows was carried on in a methodical fashion. Such lists may have been kept from the very beginning of the practice in the church to support widows (cf. Acts 6). It is difficult to suppose that Paul as a practical man should contemplate an order of "ecclesiastical widows" whose members would first enter upon their duties at the late age of sixty, an age relatively more advanced in the East than in the West. If they constitute a definite official order we would have expected a mention of them in connection with the deaconesses. In view of Paul's instructions concerning younger widows, it seems best to regard them as widows whom the Church judged worthy to be enrolled among those being given full support in comfort and honor. That they had a ministry to render is obvious, but it was not an official ministry, but rather a personal ministry of love, counsel, and prayer.

a) The qualifications of those enrolled, vv. 9, 10. Paul specifies qualifications as to age and character for those to be enrolled. They must not be "under three score years old." This does not mean that widows younger than this should not receive support whenever necessary. It is assumed that those under sixty would be able to work and to support themselves or would at most need only occasional support. Those sixty or over, being genuine widows, would receive full support.

Two character qualifications are demanded. "Having been the wife of one man" means that she has lived chastely in the marriage relation. It does not mean that she must have married only once. Then Paul's instructions to the younger to remarry would bar them from support in old age. "Well reported of for good works" points to her beneficent activities as a Christian wife and mother. Such good works show that she is worthy and deserving of church support in her destitute and widowed old age. Examples of her good works, characteristic of a devout wife and mother, are indicated. That activities arising out of the discharge of commonplace duties are viewed as "good works" shows the apostle's sanctified common sense. Five examples are given. The repetition of "if" points to the lead questions to be asked in examining the worthiness of a widow for enrollment.

"If she hath brought up children" is naturally the first question and looks to her success as a Christian mother. The bearing and rearing of godly children in a Christian home is the first and greatest service of a Christian mother. "If she hath used hospitality" points to a duty constantly insisted upon for believers in the New Testament. The reference is to the ready co-operation of the wife in entertaining strangers in the home. "If she hath washed the saints' feet" is meant literally. In Eastern lands, where only sandals were worn, this was a common and necessary feature of hospitality, but it was a menial service, usually performed by the slaves. It is eloquent testimony that she was not too proud to stoop to render this service to the "saints" who came into her home. "The beautiful incident of John 13:2-17 led to an *imitatio Christi,* and the act was perpetuated as a test of Christian character" (Pope). "If she hath relieved the afflicted" may mean that she possessed means in those days, but even the poor can find many ways to minister to the needs of others out of love. However, the relief may not have been merely, or even chiefly, by gifts but by her loving and sisterly encouragement, being ever ready to mourn with those who mourn, deeming none too low or degraded to receive her ministrations of love, none outside the scope of her kindly help and counsel. "If she hath diligently followed every good work" is in the nature of a summary statement, boundless in its scope, to include any other aspects of her good works. The meaning is not that she must have distinguished herself in all of these areas of activity. They are representative of her past life as one actively engaged in "the pursuit of good works whether initiated by others or by oneself" (Bernard).

b) The rejection of the young widows, vv. 11-13. Paul next deals with other widows who, though apparently worthy of support, should not be enrolled. He commands Timothy to refuse the application of the younger widows for admission to the roll (v. 11a) and indicates his reasons for the command (vv. 11b-13).

(1) The command to reject the young widows, v. 11a. "But younger widows refuse." While relief would be given to them as necessity arose, no young widow was to be placed on the roll for permanent support. The refusal relates not to their person but to their request for admission to the roll.

(2) The reasons for the rejection, vv. 11b-13. With an explanatory "for" Paul shows that this command is not arbitrarily given. His real reason for the restriction is not the conservation of the financial resources of the church but the spiritual welfare of its members. To place these youthful widows on the roll for permanent support would be to expose them to special temptations whose subtle operations Paul had witnessed.

"When they have waxed wanton against Christ, they desire to marry; having condemnation, because they have rejected their first pledge." Those who regard the list as referring to an ecclesiastical order usually interpret this to mean that the enrollment was accompanied by a vow or pledge, either explicit or implied, to perpetual widowhood and that subsequent marriage to another husband is treachery against Christ to whom she has pledged her life. This view seems implied in the rendering "their first pledge" in the American Standard Version. But Len-

ski aptly remarks: "This is not an apostolic beginning of monastic orders. Paul is not in one breath keeping widows from
remarriage, and in the next breath urging this very thing." The
Greek word *pistis* has the meaning of pledge only in rare cases
where the context makes it clear. The expression is literally
"their first faith," and we believe that the word has its usual
theological meaning here.

"When" is literally "whenever" and implies no more than
that cases of this kind may be expected to occur. The verb "wax
wanton," taking up the thought of the prodigal living mentioned in verse 6, means that they have come to the place where
they become restive and cast off restraint, indulging in a spirit
and conduct in opposition to Christ. This restiveness expresses
itself in the desire to marry, and this becomes so strong that
instead of waiting to "marry in the Lord" they forsake their
Christian faith and marry a pagan. They become pagans again
to suit a pagan husband, thus their "first faith" is rejected,
thrown aside, for a second (false) faith. Such a second marriage
outside the Church by one whom the church had welcomed and
treated so generously would be a painful and humiliating experience for the faithful members.

Other youthful widows, if placed on the list for support,
would be exposed to the danger of developing harmful habits
and practices. "And withal they learn also to be idle, going
about from house to house." To relieve them of the necessity
of self-support would be to expose them to the dangers of idleness with all its attendant evils. "Idleness," it has well been said,
"is the teacher of every sin." In their idleness they would wander
from house to house without good cause and in doing so would
fall into the snare of becoming "tattlers also and busybodies."
They would become gossips, indulging in frivolous and harmful
conversation, and carry from house to house mischievous matters. Having no proper employment of their own they would
become "busybodies," prying into the business of others which

was none of their business. Such spiritual dangers Paul would avoid by his refusal to give them full support. Harvey remarks:

> The inspired pen has here drawn the true picture of many an idle and worse than wasted life, degrading, bemiring itself in the filthy slime of social gossip and scandal, instead of ennobling and elevating itself in the service of Christ.

c) The apostolic directive for young widows, vv. 14, 15. The words "I desire" carry the note of authority as an apostolic directive. "Therefore" reminds us that it is given with a view to avoid the dangers mentioned before. Verse 14 states the content of the directive, while verse 15 gives the justification for it.

"That the younger *widows* marry" implies of course that it is "in the Lord." The original expresses no noun, leaving us free to insert either "women" or "widows." The latter is more consistent with the context. Paul desires that the young widows remarry and take up the duties of a normal married life, "bear children, rule the household." Children complete the home and no home is complete without them. To "bear children" implies their training as well, although that would be included in "rule the household." The management of the household affairs is the particular domain of the woman. The application here of this word to the woman is interesting, since in the Gospels the ruler of the household is always the man (Matt. 13:27; 21:33; Mark 14:14, etc.). Liddon remarks: "The application of such a word to the Christian wife implies the new and improved position which was secured to women by the Gospel" (quoted by Brown). In thus living as a faithful wife and mother she will "give no occasion to the adversary for reviling." The "adversary" may here mean any human opponent of the Gospel who would be anxious to use any scandal as a means of discrediting the Gospel. But with the article the reference may well be to the personal Devil using the human adversary as his agent.

Verse 15 justifies the directive, "for already some are turned aside after Satan." The apparent harshness of Paul toward young widows is justified from his observation of actual instances. Paul conceived of the home as the woman's intended sphere, the place where she finds her security from social dangers; there her womanly qualities find their full play and receive their happiest gratification.

3) The duty of a believing woman, v. 16. With this verse the apostle rounds out the subject of support to widows by touching upon a matter not directly mentioned before. "If any woman that believeth hath widows, let her relieve them." The reading in the King James Version, "any man or woman," lacks manuscript authority; apparently the addition was made due to a failure to understand Paul's thought in this verse. He is thinking of those cases where only the wife was a Christian, or, as in the case of Lydia, where a widow herself had a family and managed a household. Such a believing woman with the means at her command is to supply the needs of any widows within her own relationship. This will leave the church finances free to be used to support those who have no other means of support. The first obligation of this believing woman is to those within her own circle. Personal charity cannot effectively be replaced by organizational charity.

c. The duty toward elders, 5:17-25. Paul next instructs Timothy in regard to his dealings with the elders in the churches and his personal bearing as requisite to this. He sets forth the duty to honor elders who do their work well (vv. 17, 18), instructs Timothy concerning the trial of an elder (vv. 19-21), advises him concerning the ordination of elders (v. 22), adds a parenthetical word of advice to Timothy about his use of a little wine (v. 23), and concludes with an enunciation of some basic principles for the testing of candidates (vv. 24, 25).

1) The duty of honoring good elders, vv. 17-18. Here the term "elder" does not mean an elderly man, as in 5:1, but a

presiding official in the church. Paul insists that elders who do their work well shall be appropriately honored (v. 17) and substantiates the demand with Scripture (v. 18).

a) The statement of the duty, v. 17. "Let the elders that rule well be counted worthy of double honor." One function of elders is seen in the words "that rule well." The elder who distinguishes himself by ruling or presiding "well" or "excellently" over the congregation is to be "counted worthy of double honor." Such honor is their due and the congregation should not be remiss in this matter through their failure properly to express their appreciation for his work. The "double honor" apparently means the honor which comes to him on account of his office and that which he obtains by fulfilling his office well.

A second function of the elders is indicated in the words "especially those who labor in the word and in teaching." This does not mean, as some suppose, that there were two kinds of elders, ruling elders and teaching elders. The qualifications required in the men to be appointed to the office show that both functions were to be united in one person (3:2, 4, 5). They were to be "apt to teach" as well as able to rule well. In the New Testament both functions are seen combined in the elders. (See I Thess. 5:12; Acts 20:20-35; Heb. 13:7, 17). Naturally some would manifest greater ability and zeal in one while others excelled in the other. Those who distinguished themselves in both were to be duly recognized. Laboring or toiling in them to the point of weariness and fatigue, they richly deserved "double honor." The word "honor" here has its primary meaning of honor and esteem, "although we may grant that the apostle was thinking particularly of the honor which the church was bound to show to their elders by presenting them with the means necessary for their support" (Huther). Compare our use of *honorarium* for a fee.

b) The substantiation of the duty, v. 18. "For the scripture saith'" is the ordinary Pauline formula of citation from the Old

Testament (Rom. 4:3; 9:17; 10:11; Gal. 4:30; I Thess. 5:18).
The substantiating quotation, introduced by "for," is from Deu-
teronomy 25:4 and is designed to set forth the duty of support
for those who labor in the ministry. Paul simply cites the Old
Testament quotation, leaving the reader to draw the inference.
The idea in the quotation is clearly expressed in the following
words, "And, the laborer is worthy of his hire." These words
appear verbatim in Luke 10:7 from the lips of Jesus. The claim
that Paul is quoting from the Gospel of Luke as Scripture need
not be maintained. But an unprejudiced reading of the verse
would imply that by "and" Paul does co-ordinate the words
with the Old Testament quotation. Apparently Paul is quoting
the words as an oral saying of Jesus, current among believers
(cf. Acts 20:35), and regards them as of equal force with the
Old Testament. Others regard the words simply as Paul's own
explanatory statement.

2) The instructions concerning the trial of an elder, vv. 19-
21. Keenly aware that even elders are not exempt from temptation and sin, Paul instructs Timothy concerning his action with
those who do fail. He advises him to use great caution in receiving an accusation against an elder (v. 19), is told to reprove
the sinning (v. 21), and is solemnly urged to be strictly im-
partial in his judgment in such cases (v. 22).

a) The caution in receiving an accusation against an elder,
v. 19. Due to misunderstanding, party faction, or personal ani-
mosity an elder at times receives the very opposite of the honor
due him. He may be accused of personal sin or doctrinal error.
Such charges Timothy is to receive with all due caution. "Against
an elder receive not an accusation, except at the mouth of two
or three witnesses." When such accusations against an elder are
brought to Timothy he must not entertain them and start judicial proceedings against the elder, unless two or three responsible
witnesses attest the charge. "The influence of even the best minister might be destroyed, if idle gossip and social tattling were

accounted a sufficient ground for serious charges and judicial proceedings" (Harvey).

b) The judgment upon the sinning, v. 20. "Them that sin reprove in the sight of all, that the rest also may be in fear." The absence of a connecting word leads many to think that Paul here changes from the subject of an offending elder to sinners generally. The statement is general enough to apply to all who sin publicly, but the context favors the limitation of the thought to the elders. Paul is thinking of cases where the charges against an elder are substantiated. Apparently the sin in view is personal, although the reference might be to the false teaching which an elder is perpetuating. "Them that sin" translates a present participle and the tense naturally suggests that they are living in the practice of sin. Such elders, convicted of sin, Timothy is to "reprove in the sight of all," that is, in the presence of all his fellow elders. The verb "reprove" may be translated "convict" and unites "the sharp convincing proof of the error and the sharp condemning reproof of the vice" (Humphreys). "That the rest also may be in fear." Some limit the meaning of "the rest" to the fellow elders, but it seems better to refer it to the church generally. "A public rebuke in such case would at once vindicate the church from complicity with the sin, and deter others from falling into it" (Harvey).

c) The impartiality in the judgment, v. 21. Fully aware of the awful responsibility of the judicial functions laid upon Timothy, Paul with great solemnity charges him to exercise judgment with complete impartiality. "I charge thee in the sight of God, and Christ Jesus, and the elect angels." It would be difficult to think of words carrying greater solemnity. Timothy is to carry out his task under the consciousness of working under the direct gaze of the spiritual world. All Christian work should be carried out as in God's sight. The use of one article with both "God and Christ Jesus" unites them, both being Deity, while another article with "the elect angels" sets them in contrast as creatures. "The elect angels" are the unfallen angels, as opposed to "the angels which kept not their first estate" (Jude 6, King James).

Paul solemnly urges Timothy "that thou observe these things without prejudice, doing nothing by partiality." "These things" refer to the preceding disciplinary instructions. "Without prejudice" points out that he is not to prejudge a case unfavorably without making a calm and careful investigation of the evidence. He must also avoid the opposite error, "doing nothing by partiality." The literal meaning of "partiality" is "leaning or inclining toward," hence points out that besetting sin of judges of being favorably inclined or biased toward one party in the trial.

3) The advice concerning the ordination of elders, v. 22. "Lay hands hastily on no man." Some understand the reference to be to the imposition of hands on reconciled offenders at their readmission into the church fellowship. This was the practice in the third century but there is no proof that it was practiced in the apostolic church. It is better with most interpreters, ancient and modern, to refer it to the ordination of elders. Timothy is not to ordain an elder "hastily," without due inquiry and deliberation. "Neither be partaker of other men's sins." Since the laying on of his hands implied his approval of and blessing upon the one ordained, to ordain unworthy men would be to tax himself with their sins, partaking of their sins through apparent approval. On the contrary, "keep thyself pure," so that he will remain fit to rebuke the sins of others. "Pure" must not be limited to moral purity, chastity, but refers rather to his purity of intention and singleness of life.

4) The suggestion concerning Timothy's use of a little wine, v. 23. "Be no longer a drinker of water, but use a little wine for thy stomach's sake and thine often infirmities." This verse comes in here as a surprise, and the connection with the context or its dislocation have been much discussed. Some think that the

words are intended to keep Timothy from drawing an inference of a false asceticism from the preceding admonition to keep himself pure. It seems best simply to regard the advice as due to Paul's fatherly concern for the health of Timothy, "prompted perhaps by the thought of the ceaseless work and consequent waste of nervous energy to which his position exposed him" (Lilley). Its presence here, whatever the explanation, is the best assurance of the authenticity of the letter. As Spence says:

> No ecclesiastical forger of the second or third century would have dreamed, or, had he dreamed, would have dared to weave into the complicated tapestry of such an Epistle such a charge as "Drink no longer water, but use a little wine—considering thine often infirmities."

The words imply that Timothy was a total abstainer from wine. Perhaps the reason was that by his example he sought to deter others from the use of this enslaving and destructive drink. Paul advises him to drink "a little wine" as well as water. The purpose of Paul's counsel was hygienic. It was apparently the best known remedy for Timothy's troubles. "Wine was one of the chief remedial agents of those times in which the science of medicine was in its infancy among Greek physicians" (Wuest). No sanction for the habit of drinking wine as a beverage can be drawn from these words. "The very injunction of Paul implies that he regarded wine as a medicine for the infirm, and not as a beverage for the strong" (Horton).

5) The enunciation of principles for testing candidates, vv. 24, 25. Following the parenthetical statement in verse 23, Paul resumes and closes the discussion concerning elders. The principles, set forth for Timothy's personal use, reveal Paul's keen insight into human nature. These principles would aid Timothy, in judging character, to avoid the danger mentioned in verse 22. In testing men as to their fitness for office, he must remember that there are two classes of sins, open and hidden. "Some men's

sins are evident, going before unto judgment." Some sins are open and manifest to all and are like heralds going before the sinner proclaiming his guilt. "And s...ie men also they follow after." In other cases the sins of men are concealed; they lag behind and are revealed only after the culprit has been thoroughly examined. The "judgment" here is not the final judgment of God, although that lies in the background, but rather the trial which Timothy must hold before candidates are appointed. The final revelation of a man's sins before the bar of God would not help Timothy now in his evaluation of a man's character.

This distinction between the open and the hidden also applies to good works. "There are good works that are evident." They are of such a character that they are known to all and distinctly reveal the inner being of the doer. "And such as are otherwise cannot be hid." There are other good works which are not conspicuous or well known but if full investigation is made they will be revealed. "This is said as a consolation to Timothy, in case he should be troubled by the thought that the doers of many good works would remain perhaps unknown to him, and might thus be overlooked in the choice of presbyters in the church" (Van Oosterzee).

d. The instructions concerning the slaves, 6:1, 2. Slaves formed a considerable element in all the apostolic churches. The very difficulty of their position made it necessary that Timothy direct special instructions to them. The dignity and spiritual freedom which they enjoyed in the Christian assembly must not blind them to the fact that Christianity did not liberate them from their obligations arising out of their status in a pagan society. They must be warned against any abuse of Christian liberty and brotherhood. White observes:

> The politico-social problem of the first ages of Christianity was the relation of freemen to slaves, just as the corresponding prob-

lem before the Church in our own day is the relation of the white to the colored races. The grand truth of the brotherhood of man is the revolutionary fire which Christ came to cast upon earth. Fire, if it is to minister to civilization, must be so controlled as to be directed. So with the social ethics of Christianity; the extent to which their logical consequences are pressed must be calculated by common sense.

In this brief paragraph Paul points out the proper attitude of Christian slaves toward their pagan masters (v. 1), indicates the relation they are to have toward Christian masters (v. 2a), and concludes with an admonition to Timothy to teach these things (v. 2b).

1) The duty of slaves toward unbelieving masters, v. 1. "Let as many as are servants under the yoke count their own masters worthy of all honor." The words "under the yoke" point to the oppressive character of the institution of slavery. "The heathen estimate of a slave differed in degree, not in kind, from their estimate of cattle" (White). The word "servants," the regular word for slaves, stands in correlation with "masters," the word denoting those who have absolute control and unrestricted power. Such was the position of the slaveowner in regard to his slaves.

As Christians these slaves are to "count their own masters worthy of all honor." They are to have an inner attitude of genuine respect for their masters which finds outward expression in word, manner, and conduct. "That a slave should serve for love and not for fear is the revolution wrought by the Gospel, which ultimately abolishes slavery" (Horton). The Christian slave's motive must be "that the name of God and the doctrine be not blasphemed." His concern for the honor of God and the doctrine which he has accepted must increase his zeal for his master's service. For Christian slaves to show themselves as disobedient and rebellious would immediately discredit Christianity with their masters and brand the new religion as subversive to society. For slaves by their conduct to cause the name of God to be blasphemed would be a deep-dyed sin.

2) The duty of the slave of a believer, v. 2a. For slaves to have Christian masters would be less frequent. Paul warns, in that case "let them not despise them," and the reason is "because they are brethren." The fact that the master is also a believer must not be a pretext to "despise" or "think down on, disdain" them but should rather promote greater respect and better service. "Let them rather serve them." A slave is under obligation to render service to any master. The fact that his master is a Christian should inspire him to render even better service, since the one who receives "the benefit" of his hearty service is "believing and beloved."

3) The duty of Timothy to teach these things, v. 2b. "These things teach and exhort." "These things" is best regarded as relating to these instructions concerning slaves. He is to continue to teach and urge these things, thus making them the accepted ethical doctrine concerning slaves in the churches. The welfare of the church was involved. "It was the duty of Timothy to teach and guard the Christian slaves against the doctrine and spirit of servile insurrection, then so widely and disastrously threatening the foundations of society in the Roman world" (Harvey).

IV. THE CONCLUDING INSTRUCTIONS AND EXHORTATIONS TO TIMOTHY, 6:3-21

WITH CHAPTER 6:3 we begin the fourth and final main division of the Epistle. The attempt directly to tie the opening verses of this division to the preceding little paragraph about the slaves is unsatisfactory. This is not merely a denunciation of men who are teaching slaves something different than Timothy is to teach them. Paul is again reverting to the false teachers dealt with in the first division. In this concluding division Paul offers Timothy his final instructions and exhortations. In it we have a description of the false teacher (vv. 3-5), a discussion of the relation of godliness and wealth (vv. 6-10), an exhortation to Timothy to live an active life in view of Christ's return (vv. 11-16), a statement of the charge to be given those who are rich (vv. 17-19), and a final appeal to Timothy personally (vv. 20, 21a).

1. The Description of the False Teacher, vv. 3-5

In chapter 1 Paul charged Timothy to stop the work of the false teachers. Here he emphasizes rather the identification of the false teacher (v. 3) and indicates the verdict which must rightly be pronounced on such men (vv. 4, 5).

a. The identification of the false teacher, v. 3. In saying, "If any man," Paul again leaves the false teacher unnamed but he clearly indicates the identifying marks of such a teacher. He is to be identified positively and negatively by what he does and what he refuses to do. The conditional form of the sentence (first class) assumes that there are such men. The positive identifying mark is that he "teacheth a different doctrine." (See on 1:3, the only other place where this verb occurs.) The mark is that he teaches doctrine diverse and incongruous to the Gospel. Negatively, he "consenteth not to sound words." The verb "consenteth" literally means "to come to, to draw near," and pictures the act of one who confidingly accepts another's offer. The false teacher refuses to accept the "sound" or "healthful" words of the Gospel being offered him. These healthful words are appositionally described as "the words of our Lord Jesus Christ." The reference is not to the words spoken directly by Him, but to the words spoken through His prophets and apostles and having their source in Him. Only here and in 6:14, according to the true text, does the order "our Lord Jesus Christ," so familiar from Paul's other writings, occur in this Epistle. The false teacher further refuses to accept "the doctrine which is according to godliness," doctrine in accord with and tending to godliness. True doctrine is inseparable from and conducive to godliness.

b. The verdict on the false teacher, vv. 4, 5. Upon such a man Paul pronounces a severe verdict. "He is puffed up," in a state of being blinded by his immense conceit (see on 3:6). He is characterized by silly ignorance, "knowing nothing." His knowledge, upon which he presumes, is limited to fables and misinterpretations of the law (cf. 1:4-7) and does not penetrate into the truth. The Williams' translation draws the two together and renders "he is a conceited ignoramus."[1] Further, he is described as "doting about questionings and disputes of words." He is "word-sick," and the morbid state of his mind manifests

[1] Charles B. Williams, *The New Testament, A Private Translation in the Language of the People* (Moody Press).

itself in subtle discussions and angry disputes centering around trifling distinctions between different words.

Paul enumerates five social consequences which flow from such a mentally diseased condition: 1) "envy," "secret annoyance at the success of their rivals in the same futile efforts" (Brown); 2) "strife," as they vie with and contradict each other; 3) "railings," or "blasphemies," vehement denunciations couched in sacred words; 4) "evil surmisings," "malicious suspicions as to the honesty of those who differ with them" (White); 5) "wranglings," persistent and obstinate frictions among the contenders.

Sadder still is the spiritual character of the men who are occupied with such teaching. They are "men corrupted in mind and bereft of the truth." Their "mind," the organ of moral thinking and comprehension, is in a state of corruption and disintegration, no longer functioning normally. "When meeting 'the truth' the corrupted mind sees and seeks only objections, when meeting what differs from this truth it sees and seeks reasons for accepting this difference" (Lenski). Thus they have become and are now in a state of being "bereft of the truth." "The truth was once theirs; they have disinherited themselves" (White). Such men are capable of erroneously "supposing that godliness is a way of gain." They conceived of their show of godliness as a profitable commercial investment, a lucrative business, advancing one's worldly interests. The addition in the Received Text, "from such withdraw thyself," is insufficiently supported by manuscript evidence.

2. The Relation of Godliness and Wealth, vv. 6-10

The error of the false teachers leads Paul into a discussion of the relation between godliness and wealth. Paul repudiates the perverted concept that godliness is a means of advancing one's material interests, but he knows that there is a sense in which it is a great gain, even in this life. He sets forth the condition under which godliness is gain (vv. 6-8), and by contrast points out the danger to those seeking wealth (vv. 9, 10).

a. The gain of true godliness, vv. 6-8. In considering godliness as true gain he shows that it is such when connected with contentment (v. 6) and proceeds to elucidate the nature of Christian contentment (vv. 7, 8).

1) The gain of godliness with contentment, v. 6. "But" introduces the contrast between the erroneous view of the false teachers and the Christian view. "Godliness with contentment is great gain." The verb "is" stands emphatically forward, such is actually the case, Paul insists, when it is combined with an inner attitude of contentment. "Contentment" is literally "self-sufficiency." A state of contentment makes one independent of outward circumstances, satisfied with one's inner resources, enabling one to maintain a spiritual equilibrium in the midst of favorable as well as unfavorable circumstances. It is not a stoical indifference to or contempt for material needs. The Christian can be self-sufficient because his sufficiency is rooted and grounded in God's all-sufficiency and rests with assurance upon God's providential care. Such contentment naturally belongs to true godliness. "S. Paul knows that man is only satisfied in God; and therefore devotion to God is the first condition of this true satisfaction, and contentedness with an earthly lot the second" (Liddon, quoted in Brown). Such godliness is a very different thing from the mercenary concept of the false teachers. It is truly "great gain." It not only brings satisfaction amid one's earthly lot but fills the soul with positive good. "Godliness makes us content, and to be content is the highest good" (Van Oosterzee).

2) The nature of godly contentment, vv. 7, 8. With "for" Paul elucidates the nature of this godly contentment, now restated in personal terms. (Notice the three "we" verbs.) As believers we realize the transitoriness and perishableness of all that this world gives. It is an indisputable fact that "we brought

nothing into the world." "Not a thing" (emphatic by position) did we bring in at birth, "neither can we carry anything out." Since after a brief stay we shall go out as we came in, it is folly to be anxious and preoccupied with merely earthly things. Our chief concern in this life is with eternal spiritual realities, and so we are prepared to be satisfied with the supply of our personal wants. "Having food and covering we shall be therewith content." The word translated "covering" is general enough to include both clothing and shelter, but the immediate context favors limiting it to personal possessions such as dress. Both of the words "food and covering" are plural in the original, "indicating 'supplies of,' for each mouth to be fed, each household to be clothed" (Humphreys). The future passive "we shall be therewith content" is not an implied exhortation, urging believers to be content, but rather an assertion of realized contentment. Whatever may have been our previous attitude, this is what we will do henceforth. Whatever may be granted above our actual needs will be thankfully received, but the earnest and devout Christian will be satisfied when his actual needs are supplied.

b. The danger to those seeking wealth, vv. 9, 10. With a contrasting "but" Paul shows what happens to people who do not have this attitude of Christian contentment but are determined to gain wealth. He indicates the nature of their danger (v. 9), states the reason for the danger (v. 10a), and points out the verification of the danger from actual life (v. 10b).

1) The nature of the danger, v. 9. "They that are minded to be rich fall into a temptation and a snare." They have made the acquisition of wealth the considered aim and purpose of their lives. Their eagerness to amass wealth causes them repeatedly to "fall into temptation," the temptation to neglect the highest interests of the soul and to stoop to improper means to obtain wealth. Their striving becomes a "snare" or trap into which they fall, finding themselves held by "many foolish and hurtful

lusts." They find themselves chained by lusts which prove to be "foolish," because they do not yield the promised satisfaction, and are positively "hurtful," because they destroy that which is noblest and best in them, making them envious, avaricious, and hardhearted in their unscrupulous dealings. The consequence of these lusts is that "they drown men in destruction and perdition." The term "destruction" is general, pointing to the ruin of body or soul, while "perdition" points mainly to the utter loss of the soul in eternity. The word translated "drown" is literally "sink"; it gives the picture of these lusts overwhelming the man, like the waves covering a sinking ship, and plunging him into perdition.

2) The reason for the danger, v. 10a. That such disastrous effects come from the desire to be rich is due to the fact that "the love of money is a root of all kinds of evil." The absence of the definite article with "root" shows that the love of money is not the only root of evil, but is one of its most common and prolific sources. "There is no kind of evil that the craving for wealth may not originate, once its roots become fairly planted in the soil of the heart" (Lilley). The connotation in "the love of money" (*philarguria*) is not the acquisition of wealth in order that it may be used in prodigal expenditure but rather the miserly accumulation and hoarding of money for the very love of it. That which should be a means to support life is made the end of life itself.

3) The verification of the danger, v. 10b. The tragic facts of actual experience verify the danger. "Which [that is, the money itself, not merely the love of it] some reaching after have been led astray from the faith." Paul's observant eye had sadly noted how certain people in "reaching after," eagerly stretching themselves out after money, "have been led astray," made to wander away from the straight path of "the faith." The Christian faith which they once professed has become displaced by their love for money as the chief goal of their lives. Added

to this fateful negative loss is the positive damage of self-in-flicted sorrow, "and have pierced themselves through with many sorrows." In their eagerness to pluck the fair flower of wealth they have pierced and wounded themselves with its sharp, un-suspected thorns. A condemning conscience assails them and destroys their happiness, while they suffer under their poignant disillusionment.

3. The Exhortation to an Active Life in View of Christ's Return, vv. 11-16

Paul again turns to Timothy personally with an exhortation to an active life in view of Christ's return. It is the only safe antidote to the perils just pictured. This stirring passage forms the real climax of the Epistle. In it we have a remarkable characterization of the person addressed (v. 11a), the statement of the specific duties urged upon him (vv. 11b, 12), and an elaborate restatement of the charge to Timothy (vv. 13-16).

a. The characterization of the one addressed, v. 11a. "But thou" sets Timothy in contrast to those who fall into destructive perils through their desire to get wealth. He is further addressed as "O man of God." The "O" is seldom used in Greek in direct address and is therefore all the more impressive. "Man of God" is the regular designation for a prophet in the Old Testament. Some think that the application of this Old Testament title to Timothy suggests that he had similar privileges and responsibilities. In II Timothy 3:17, the only other place in the New Testament where the expression occurs, it undoubtedly has a general connotation as indicative of a mature Christian. The epithet can be applied to any mature believer standing in a place of leadership responsibility. The following exhortations show that Paul is thinking of Timothy's position as a responsible Christian. It marks him as a man belonging to God, a man removed from the realm of the merely temporal, transitory, and perishing things of this world.

b. The statement of the specific duties, vv. 11b, 12. The duties indicated are both negative and positive. "Flee these things," that is, the love of money and its attendant evils. The tense stresses the continuing duty, "Be ever fleeing," never let them catch you; the margin of safety can never be too great. But the Christian life is more than just avoiding the evils of the world; there must also be the constant pursuit of positive virtues. "And follow after righteousness, godliness, faith, love, patience, meekness." The negative was briefly stated, but the positive activity is elaborated in the enumeration of six virtues, named in three pairs, which must be actively and energetically pursued. "Righteousness, godliness" point to the attitude of the soul toward God. The former designates the conformity in character to the divine will in purpose, thought, and action, while the latter denotes the devotion to God in reverence and worship. "Faith, love" are the fountal source of the Christian life. "The one may be termed the hand that lays hold of God's mercy; and the other the mainspring of the Christian's life" (Spence). "Patience, meekness" look outward and set forth the disposition necessary in those who encounter the antagonism of a Christ-rejecting world. The former denotes a steadfast endurance of life's trials and persecutions, while the latter expresses that meekness of disposition which makes no high claims for itself nor strenuously insists upon its own rights.

The Christian life demands strenuous effort. "Fight the good fight of the faith, lay hold on the life eternal." The figure, a favorite one with Paul, is not drawn from the battlefield, as our translations suggest, but from the athletic arena. "Be contending the good contest" pictures Timothy as an athlete striving for the prize. "The faith" is objective, as the article indicates; the acceptance of the Christian faith always involves a conflict with its opponents. He must show himself a hero in the contest. "The conflict with evil, which is involved in the acceptance of Christ, is called 'good' in contradistinction to other conflicts, e.g., those of the arena, boxing, running, etc., which are without spiritual significance" (Pope). The true goal and prize of the spiritual combatant is "the eternal life." The verb "fight" is in the present tense and indicates the continuity of the struggle in this life, while the verb "lay hold" is aorist and takes us to the last supreme moment of the contest when the prize is won. "Whereunto thou wast called" drops the figure and reminds Timothy that at his conversion he was called to such a life of struggle in connection with the faith with its glorious consummation of eternal life. "And didst confess the good confession in the sight of many witnesses." Some would refer the good confession made by Timothy to some experience of persecution in his life; others think of the time of his ordination; but the combination of the confession with the call unto eternal life links it to his conversion and public confession of "the faith" at baptism.

c. The restatement of the charge, vv. 13-16. Paul supplements the call to an aggressive Christian life with a solemn charge to Timothy. His words stress the solemnity of the charge (v. 13), indicate the contents of the charge (v. 14a), and point to the termination of the charge (vv. 14b-16).

1) The solemnity of the charge, v. 13. Once again Paul represents God the Father and Christ Jesus as present and witnessing both the charge being given and the conduct of Timothy in the fulfillment of his duty (cf. 5:21). "I charge thee in the sight of God, who giveth life to all things." The reading "who giveth life to all things" pictures God as the source of all life; it would remind Timothy that should he meet death for the sake of the Gospel God is able to raise him up in the resurrection of the just. But the reading suggested in the margin, "who preserveth all things alive," is better attested. It views God as the Preserver of all, able to preserve His servant faithful even unto death in a courageous defense of the Gospel. "And of Christ Jesus, who before Pontius Pilate witnessed a good confession." The reference is to Christ's historical witness before Pilate when

He witnessed to His person and work (John 18:33-38; 19:8-11). "His confession before Pilate became the model, the motive, and the power of all the confessions which his followers make for him" (Horton).

2) The contents of the charge, v. 14a. "That thou keep the commandment, without spot, without reproach." This is the heart of the duty which Paul so solemnly lays upon Timothy. He is to "keep," that is, to preserve intact, "the commandment." The entire truth of the Gospel which he has confessed and which he has been commissioned to preach and to defend is here unified under the singular noun "commandment." It is his duty constantly to be preserving it as a priceless treasure, "without spot, without reproach." "He is to keep the commandment which is in itself spotless, and to keep it so as to expose it to no blame" (Huther).

3) The termination of the charge, vv. 14b-16. The duty that has been laid upon Timothy is not a temporary matter. The duty extends throughout the course of this present life and terminates with the return of Christ. Paul states the termination of the charge (v. 14b) and explains it (vv. 15, 16).

a) The statement of the termination, v. 14b. The responsibility to guard and proclaim the Gospel rests upon Timothy, and every true believer, "until the appearing of our Lord Jesus Christ." The reference is to the visible manifestation of Christ at His Second Advent. The word "appearing" or "manifestation" emphasizes the visibility and glory of the coming Lord who is now hidden and invisible to human sight in Heaven. This statement of the termination of the charge shows that the writer did not conceive of the return of Christ as some event in the remote future. Like the other New Testament writers, Paul kept the truth of the Lord's return in the foreground of his thinking and hopes. While Paul eagerly looked for that event, he never pretended to know the date of the return. The overwhelming magnitude of the Second Coming made it seem near and shrivel up all intervening time, like some vast mountain, which, as it rears its gigantic peak above the horizon, seems near, though actually a long distance away.

b) The explanation of the termination, vv. 14b-16. With the words "which in his own time he shall show" Paul indicates that the longed-for return of Christ as to its actual occurrence was wholly in the hands of God. The Second Advent, like the First, will occur in the time ordered and appointed by the Father. Paul's statement is not that Christ will display His appearing, but that the Father will display it. The same God that preserves all things will effect the Second Coming. This thought draws out of Paul a doxology of praise to the Father. It contains a sevenfold description of God. 1) "The blessed and only Potentate" points to the character and the universal authority of Him who will bring back Christ in open glory. "The first epithet describes the perfection of bliss enjoyed by the First Person of the Trinity; the second, the uniqueness and absoluteness of His power." (Pope). 2 and 3) "The King of kings, and Lord of lords" is descriptive of His sovereign authority and rule. He is King over all those acting as kings, and Lord over all those acting as lords over others. 4) "Who only hath immortality," that is, immortality as an essential, underived attribute. The word here rendered "immortality" is literally "deathlessness" and speaks of His absolute deathless existence. The adjective in 1:17 translated "immortal" comes from a different word which means "not liable to corruption or decay." His deathless, unchanging existence precludes any decay, corruption, or degeneration in His being. 5) "Dwelling in light unapproachable" speaks of the inaccessibility of God to human senses. He dwells in an atmosphere too glorious for mortal creatures to approach. 6 and 7) The relative clauses, "whom no man hath seen, nor can see" emphasize the essential nature of God as invisible. Finite man never has seen God in His eternal essence, nor can he do so (cf. John 1:18). "The vision of God, however, is in some sense promised to the saints (cf. Matt. 5:8; I Cor. 13:12; I John 3:2; Rev. 22:4); but such vision can never be complete sight, since in the nature of things the finite can never perfectly comprehend the Infinite" (Harvey).

To such a God Paul ascribes his praise, "to whom *be* honor and power eternal. Amen." The verb is unexpressed in the Greek. It is not a wish but an acknowledgment of fact. All esteem, reverence, adoration, worship are His due, and "strength eternal" are His in possession and exercise. The concluding "Amen" seals all that has been ascribed to God.

4. The Charge Concerning the Rich, vv. 17-19

In verse 9 above Paul dealt with those who "are minded to be rich"; to complete the subject, he now deals with those who are rich. The intervening paragraph shows that his warning to the former class does not imply any censure of the latter class. They are a distinct group in his mind. He names the group he has in view (v. 17a), sets forth the contents of the charge to be given them (vv. 17b, 18), and adds an encouragement in the carrying out of the charge (v. 19).

a. The persons to be charged, v. 17a. "Charge them that are rich" clearly implies that there were wealthy members in the church at this time. No blame is attached to that fact, for they may be rich through an inheritance, natural prosperity in business, or some other perfectly proper way. Christianity is not opposed to believers being rich, but it is vitally concerned that they have the right attitude toward their riches and make proper use of it. "Rich in this present world" sets them in contrast to other believers who, like the slaves, are poor in this present world. They need to be warned since their favored status may make it difficult for them to take a humble position in the church.

b. The contents of the charge, vv. 17b, 18. Timothy must warn these rich believers concerning the dangers which their very wealth creates for them (v. 17b) and press upon them their proper duties (v. 18).

1) Neg.—The dangers they are to avoid, v. 17b. The rich believers must be warned concerning the danger of a wrong attitude toward others and toward their wealth. "That they be not highminded" warns against the special danger of the rich in their attitude toward others. They must avoid the temptation to think themselves superior to the poor. "The pride of purse is not only vulgar, it is sinful" (Bernard). They also stand in danger of having a wrong attitude toward their wealth, "nor have their hope set on the uncertainty of riches." A notorious characteristic of wealth is that it so often takes wings and flies away, as many a formerly rich man has regretfully discovered. Hence to have placed and to continue to place their hope (perfect tense) on their wealth is to repose their hope on the very quality of wealth which least justifies it. Wealth is not a basis for a sure hope. "But," in passing to the positive, they are to set their hope "on God, who giveth us richly all things to enjoy." The unchanging God is the only sure basis for hope. "Their kind Master in heaven not only allows men reasonable pleasures and gratifications, but even Himself abundantly provides for them" (Spence). God does not provide material wealth to stimulate pride or self-exaltation but intends that His gifts be used and enjoyed with all gratitude.

2) Pos.—The duties they are to fulfill, v. 18. That Paul is not thinking of any selfish gratification in the use of wealth is shown by the positive duties he sets before the rich. Four duties, named in pairs, are indicated. "That they do good, that they be rich in good works." The present tense names them as continuing duties. They are to live lives of holy beneficence and are to use their wealth as a means for the performance of noble deeds in abundance. This is the way in which the rich may truly enjoy their wealth. The second pair gives specific points, "that they be ready to distribute, willing to communicate." The former is literally "to be sharing well or generously with." It points to the personal attribute of being a generous, liberal giver, sharing with

others that which they have received from God. The second
word means one "ready and apt to form and maintain communion and fellowship," thus pointing out that the rich believer must
not hold aloof from his poor brethren but must be willing to
accept and treat them as equals.

c. The encouragement in carrying out the charge, v. 19. They
are to find encouragement to persevere in such a life of active
beneficence from the fact of the reward thus secured for the
future. "Laying up in store for themselves a good foundation
against the time to come." By their use of their wealth for good
deeds they are "laying up" or accumulating spiritual treasures
for themselves in Heaven. "Earthly wealth, thus transmuted into
heavenly riches, is gathered as an indestructible treasure awaiting
the soul in the future world" (Harvey). The treasures thus
stored up form a "good foundation," a solid and stable investment for future rewards. There is no hint here of any meritorious
works which give a sinner acceptance before God. "To be chari-
table for the sake of gaining heaven by it, is absurdity, for the
selfish motive vitiates the act" (Washburn, in Van Oosterzee).
Rather, such good works are the evidence of faith and justification and as such assure us that we now possess genuine spiritual
life. They also give us the assurance of a glorious future consummation, "that they may lay hold on the life which is life indeed."
As in 6:12, the verb "lay hold" is aorist and takes us to the final
realization of "the life which is life indeed." The manuscript
authority is strongly in favor of the adverb "really" or "indeed"
instead of the adjective "eternal" used in the King James Version. "The contrast is thus between selfish, worldly living as not
real life, and unselfish, beneficent living as that which is true life,
in its proper idea and end" (Harvey). "The life which is life
indeed" has its beginning on this side of the grave and finds its
consummation on the other side of the grave.

5. The Final Appeal to Timothy, vv. 20, 21a

The Epistle closes with a serious and affectionate appeal to

Timothy, being in reality a summary of its entire contents. Timothy is urged to keep unscathed the sacred deposit that has been entrusted to him in the face of all adversaries. Paul indicates the positive duty of Timothy (v. 20a) as well as the negative safeguard (vv. 20b, 21a).

a. The positive appeal to guard the deposit, v. 20a. The summary statement of Timothy's duty is to "guard that which is committed unto thee." The Greek is literally, "Guard the deposit." What the deposit is he does not say, but the tenor of the letter makes it plain that it is "the whole system of evangelic truth on the preservation of which Paul has been instructing Timothy through the epistle" (Lilley). The verb "guard" raises the picture of a soldier standing guard over a treasure which has been committed to him for safekeeping. The aorist tense urges its effective accomplishment. The word of the truth of the Gospel is the minister's chief treasure which he must not part with or suffer to be mixed with elements foreign to its nature and purpose.

b. The safeguard in rejecting the spurious, vv. 20b, 21a. On the negative side Timothy will find his safety in a habitual refusal to give heed to the matter and methods of the false teachers. He is constantly to be "turning away from the profane babblings and oppositions of the knowledge which is falsely so-called." These things he must avoid. The mention of "profane babblings" takes us back to 1:4-7 and once more reminds us of the utter hollowness and emptiness of the false teaching to be combatted. The use of the one article closely unites the "profane babblings" with the "oppositions of knowledge which is false so-called." The word "oppositions" denotes the opposing positions and arguments of the false teachers. These oppositions were paraded with a vaunted claim to superior "knowledge." "The knowledge" claimed was supposed to be superior to that given by the Gospel. With crushing effect Paul designates such knowledge "falsely so-called." It has a show of learning but it is a misnomer. It was in reality the enemy of the faith.

The concluding relative clause constitutes a warning in that it shows the inevitable result of following such spurious knowledge. "Which some professing have erred concerning the faith." The false teachers are again referred to indefinitely as "some" or "certain ones." Their profession of such teaching has had the tragic effect that they "have erred concerning the faith." Literally, they "have missed the mark" (same word translated "having swerved" in 1:6) as regards "the faith." "The faith" is objective and denotes the doctrinal content of the Christian faith. By their professed adherence to this spurious teaching they have tragically strayed from the path of Christian truth. Their example constitutes a solemn warning which Timothy must hold up before the congregations.

THE BENEDICTION
6:21b

"Grace be with you."

The word "grace" has the article in the Greek and means the well-known "grace of the Lord Jesus Christ" mentioned in most of the earlier Pauline benedictions. The manuscripts are divided on the singular "thee" and the plural "you," but the latter is better attested. Thus the benediction is not only to Timothy but includes, in Paul's thought, all those with whom Timothy is dealing as the apostolic representative.

BIBLIOGRAPHY ON I TIMOTHY

Alford, Henry, *The Greek Testament*. Vol. III. London: Rivingtons (2nd ed., 1857), 117 and 416 pp.

Bernard, J. H., "The Pastoral Epistles," *Cambridge Greek Testament*. Cambridge: Cambridge University Press (1922 reprint), lxxviii and 192 pp.

Brown, Ernest Faulkner, "The Pastoral Epistles," *Westminster Commentaries*. London: Methuen & Co., Ltd. (1917), xxxiv and 121 pp.

Ellicott, Charles J., *A Critical and Grammatical Commentary on the Pastoral Epistles*. Andover: Warren F. Draper (1865), xviii and 265 pp.

Gurney, T. A., "The First Epistle to Timothy," *A Devotional Commentary*. London: The Religious Tract Society (no date), 276 pp.

Harvey, H., "Commentary on the Pastoral Epistles, First and Second Timothy and Titus; and the Epistle to Philemon," *An American Commentary on the New Testament*. Philadelphia: The American Baptist Publication Society (1890; reprint, no date), 164 pp.

Hervey, A. C., "I Timothy," *The Pulpit Commentary*. Grand Rapids: Wm. B. Eerdmans Publishing Co. (1950 reprint), 141 pp.

Horton, R. F., "The Pastoral Epistles," *The Century Bible*. London: Blackwood, Le Bas & Co. (no date), 196 pp.

Humphreys, A. E., "The Epistles to Timothy and Titus," *The Cambridge Bible for Schools*. Cambridge: Cambridge University Press (1925 reprint), 271 pp.

Huther, Joh. Ed., "Critical and Exegetical Handbook to the Epistles of St. Paul to Timothy and Titus," Meyer's *Critical and Exegetical Commentary on the New Testament*. Translated by David Hunter, Edinburgh: T. & T. Clark (1893), 379 pp.

Kelly, William, *An Exposition of the Two Epistles to Timothy.* London: C. A. Hammond (no date), xv and 348 pp.

Lenski, R. C. H., *The Interpretation of St. Paul's Epistles to the Colossians, to the Thessalonians, to Timothy, to Titus and to Philemon.* Columbus, Ohio: Lutheran Book Concern (1937), 986 pp.

Lilley, J. P., "The Pastoral Epistles," *Handbooks for Bible Classes.* Edinburgh: T. & T. Clark (1901), 255 pp.

Lipscomb, David, *A Commentary on the New Testament Epistles.* Edited, with additional Notes, by J. W. Shepherd. Nashville, Tenn.: Gospel Advocate Co. (1942), 324 pp.

Lock, Walter, "A Critical and Exegetical Commentary on the Pastoral Epistles," *The International Critical Commentary.* Edinburgh: T. & T. Clark (1924; 1936 reprint), xliv and 163 pp.

Pope, R. Martin, *The Epistles of Paul the Apostle to Timothy and Titus.* London: Charles H. Kelly (1901), 248 pp.

Spence, H. D. M., "The Pastoral Epistles of St. Paul," *Ellicott's Commentary on the Whole Bible.* Grand Rapids: Zondervan Publishing House (reprint, no date), pp. 171-264.

Van Oosterzee, J. J., "The Pastoral Epistles," "The First Epistle of Paul to Timothy," Lange *Commentary on the Holy Scriptures.* Translated by Drs. Washburn and Harwood. Grand Rapids: Zondervan Publishing House (reprint, no date), 76 pp.

White, Newport J. D., "The First and Second Epistles to Timothy and the Epistle to Titus," *The Expositor's Greek Testament.* Grand Rapids: Wm. B. Eerdmans Publishing Co. (reprint, no date), pp. 55-202.

Wuest, Kenneth S. *The Pastoral Epistles in the Greek New Testament for the English Reader.* Grand Rapids: Wm. B. Eerdmans Publishing Co (1952), 209 pp.